Acknowledgements

We would like to thank all those involved in providing social work education who made time in very busy schedules to contribute to this knowledge review by:

- providing information on research and publications pertinent to the field
- sending programme documentation and examples of education practice
- responding to telephone interviews
- participating in focus group discussion
- reading and commenting on materials.

We are indebted to the following individuals who participated as members of the Stakeholder Group, advising on the work of the Review and commenting on draft materials:

Christine Billings, Anna Chime, Jo Elsey, Katie Pound, University of Sussex social work students
Brett Bignall East Sussex Disability Association
Jenny Clifton, Voice of the Child
Clare Ockwell West Sussex CAPITAL Project
Venus Sedarous, Hove Somali Elders
Justine Stewart, Brighton and Hove Council
Chris Taylor, East Sussex Council
Russell Whiting, West Sussex Council

We are particularly appreciative of the contributions by Anna Chime, Brett Bignall, Clare Ockwell and Venus Sedarous who led focus groups on visits to four universities to explore 'good practice' in partnership work. Also to Russell Whiting who undertook some keywording on the Research Review.

We are also particularly indebted to the many social work education colleagues who submitted original material for use as practice examples and have been ready to share their work to enable the development of learning, teaching and assessment of partnership work.

London Metropolitan University
London South Bank University
University of Bath
University of Brighton
University of Hull
University of Lancaster
University of Nottingham
University of Plymouth
University of Sussex
University of Wales Institute at Cardiff

Finally, we would like to thank Mike Fisher and Fiona Macleod at the Social Care Institute for Excellence (SCIE), and David Gough and Esther Coren on behalf of the Evidence for Policy and Practice Information and Co-ordinating Centre (EPPI) who have provided invaluable support, consultation and advice throughout the project.

Summary

Background

The Social Care Institute for Excellence (SCIE) commissioned the University of Sussex, in partnership with the Evidence for Policy and Practice Information and Coordinating Centre (EPPI-Centre), to undertake a systematic review and practice survey of 'partnership' in social work education. There were nine stated objectives in the commission, including clarifying the discourse of partnership, identifying the national and international evidence and best practice in partnership work, examining how stakeholders are involved, evaluating the most effective methods of teaching, learning and assessment and evaluating the evidence on the transfer of learning and impact on learners. On some of these issues, for example the transfer of learning, there was very little evidence in either the literature or the practice. The parameters of the study included focusing on partnership at pre-qualifying level in England, Wales and Northern Ireland. This Knowledge Review is the outcome of work undertaken during October 2004-May 2005.

The regulatory framework for social work education in the UK has emerged from different sources and it is perhaps not surprising that there is a difference in whether partnership is with users and carers, other professions, or both, how it is defined and what is required. Partnership is not referred to explicitly in the *National Occupational Standards (NOS) for Social Work*. It is explicit in the *Department of Health (England) Requirements for Social Work Training* (2002), the *Qualification Framework for the Degree in Social Work in Wales* (2003), the *Northern Ireland Framework Specification for the Degree in Social Work* (2003) and the *Code of Practice for Social Care Workers* (2002). It is embedded in requirements for collaboration and interdisciplinary practice in the *Quality Assurance Authority Benchmark Statement for Social Work* (1999).

The ambiguous nature of 'partnership work' is also discussed in the literature (for example, Barr et al, 2000), with terms such as 'collaboration', 'cooperation', multi and interdisciplinary', 'multi and inter-professional' often used interchangeably. The expectation to achieve partnership is not as clear as it might be, and this study provides the opportunity for a debate about its nature.

Methodology

This study comprises a Research Review and Practice Survey. The Research Review was undertaken to SCIE standards for systematic reviewing, using tools for keywording and data extraction developed to ensure rigour at the EPPI-Centre. The EPPI-Centre (www.eppi.ioe.ac.uk) is part of the Social Science Research Unit (SSRU) at the Institute of Education in London. It has a well-established infrastructure for supporting groups undertaking systematic reviews including online tools and guidance for searching, keywording and data extraction that enable studies using the full range of methodologies to be included in the reviews. Since neither SCIE nor the Sussex team wished to exclude any studies on the basis of type of methodology alone, the EPPI-Centre tools were considered most appropriate. The systems had been used extensively for reviews in education and health promotion but not, as yet, for reviewing social work research. Hence, the Sussex team worked with the EPPI-Centre staff to extend and adapt these tools for this review.

The systematic review process involved full electronic searching of databases and websites, handsearching journals and 'grey' literature. Inclusion and exclusion criteria were defined and abstracts screened against these criteria to identify 119 articles to keyword. Crucially, given debates about the concept of partnership, studies about interprofessional education were included only where the focus was clearly on partnership work. Interprofessional education is likely to be a topic for a future SCIE Research Review. Sources beyond empirical work, such as commentaries, theoretical contributions, users' or carers' accounts and policy documents were included in the Research Review, but data extraction and detailed quality judgements were applied to relevant empirical work only. Thirteen studies that were identified as having sufficient empirical content were data extracted.

In the Practice Survey, three strategies were designed to enable a 'drilling down' approach with providers of the new degrees and their stakeholders. These included the construction of an initial 'map' or base line of partnership work undertaken by a document analysis of 33 programme handbooks (41% of programmes contacted) and nine module handbooks. Fourteen telephone interviews were undertaken with a sample of either programme directors for the new degree or convenors for modules focusing on the learning and teaching of partnership, including one in Wales, one in Northern Ireland and 12 in England. Inclusion in the sample was on the basis of 'evidence of good practice', geographic spread and a balance of undergraduate and postgraduate programmes. Focus groups were held with students (four groups), staff (four groups) and service users (three groups) in four universities in England to explore and consider partnership learning, teaching and assessment, and to establish a picture of 'good practice' in 'partnership work'.

The research team introduced criteria for good practice against which potential examples could be rated. Four criteria were identified in the original research proposal. A further three were added following discussion with the project stakeholder group.

The project stakeholder group, including practitioners, service users and carers and students, played a key role in the Research Review. They acted as consultants and 'critical friends'. Stakeholder group members, including users and carers and students, also worked as co-researchers in leading focus groups. The research strategy adopted by the Practice Survey was time and resource intensive for both researchers and participants. Access to some universities was limited by resource and time factors, since visits required considerable organisation when staff were under pressure from a number of other factors. Research fatigue among educators was also a barrier to access.

Characteristics of the studies

Overall, the 119 papers selected for inclusion in the Research Review came in equal numbers from the UK and the US, with very few from elsewhere. Of the 13 that met the criteria for data extraction, seven were from the US, five from the UK and one from Israel. The papers included in the whole Research Review were mainly focused (categories were not mutually exclusive) on interprofessional education; a high proportion overall also focused on practice learning and almost all on the academic curriculum. Eight of the data extracted studies focused on interprofessional education and five on partnership with service users and carers. Four studies were descriptive, seven were evaluations, one an exploration of relationships and descriptive, and one both descriptive and evaluative.

Key findings

In the following, 'Review' refers to findings in both the Research Review and Practice Survey.

Conceptual hybridity and confusion about partnership are rife in the theoretical literature, the empirical literature and the practice surveyed. The Knowledge Review describes the inclusion and exclusion criteria in detail, which clarifies how the concept was addressed in the Review. There is a strong commitment to partnership work in social work education, grounded in a philosophy and value base at the core of social work. This Review suggests that the concept is simultaneously contested and taken for granted. The Practice Survey found a wide variation in views of the learning, teaching and assessment of partnership work by different providers. Similarly it revealed that partnership work is more often implicit than explicit and it is regarded as self-evident that partnership will be central to learning.

A single, unambiguous definition of partnership work did not emerge from this Review. In both the Research Review (see, for example, Jackson and Morris, 1994; Julia and Kondrat, 2000) and the Practice Survey, it was clear that the concept of partnership is under-theorised and that social work education tends to draw rather minimally on conceptualisations of partnership that may be rather more developed – albeit contested – in wider spheres. In the absence of this, programmes draw on a range of related material, including for example organisation and empowerment theory. Practitioners and some researchers argue that judgements about the effectiveness of partnership can only be made if the concept is clarified and developed.

Who does partnership in social work education involve? The majority of studies in the Research Review focusing on interprofessional partnership work involve predominantly health-related professions (for example, nursing, occupational therapy, speech therapy, midwifery and general practice), with law and education only occasionally mentioned. The empirical studies show no significant differences in outcomes with, or for, different groups. However, there is some evidence (for example, Whittington and Bell, 2001) that social workers perceive particular professional groups (for example, nurses) to have a better understanding of social work roles than others (for example, doctors, police), and that these latter groups are the ones with whom they are less likely to experience shared learning.

The Research Review found that education about partnership with service users and carers embraces children and families, mental health, disability and child protection. No less attention seems to be paid to partnership in areas of social work practice that may involve some degree of social control (such as mental health) than in others, although the complexities of partnership with involuntary clients are rarely explicitly addressed. The Practice Survey identified a number of interacting relationships, which comprise the content and process of partnership education. These include service users and carers, educators, practitioners, students and other professionals. However, the greater emphasis on service user involvement in the new degree means that this aspect of partnership receives particular attention.

What does partnership in social work education include, and how is it included? The focus in studies evaluating interprofessional partnership education is on students developing an understanding of other professions and intergroup relations, recognition of role distinctions, boundaries and complementarity, understanding of common and different core knowledge and value bases, the development of collaborative, communication, networking and conflict resolution skills (Barr and Waterton, 1996a, 1996b). For partnership work with service users and carers, the emphasis is on student understanding of user and carer experiences, recognition of their worth and expertise and the reduction of discriminatory attitudes and stigma (Jackson and Morris, 1994; Shor and Sykes, 2002; Scheyett and Diehl, 2004; Elliott et al, 2005). Many of the studies included in the Research Review, and most of those data extracted for the in-depth review, focus on some of these areas. Partnership education initiatives reported in the literature to date are mainly about discrete courses or practice-based projects, many demonstrating the 'creative and inclusive methods of promoting partnership' called for by Levin (2004) on behalf of SCIE.

The Practice Survey identified two main approaches to the learning, teaching and assessment of partnership work. In the 'embedded' approach, the learning and teaching is integrated into other curricula, although this may not be explicitly stated as an aim or outcome. Linked with the notion of 'embeddedness' is a view that students learn about partnership through experiencing it modelled in programmes; an example might be a programme infrastructure that includes service user and carer or student representation. In the discrete approach, specific modules are provided focusing on aspects of partnership; these are varied in their perspective and may, for example, take an organisational or a values and anti-oppressive practice) perspective. Module convenors and students would welcome well-theorised core texts about partnership. Some programmes combine the two approaches. Each approach has a clearly articulated rationale, although this is often not stated in programme documentation. Examples of evidence of good practice in both approaches are identified in the Practice Survey.

Interprofessional education rarely appeared to involve wholesale integration. Many (for example, Colarossi and Forgey, 2006) argue for the involvement of interprofessional teams of educators as a means of 'modelling' partnership, and students highlighted this positively. The most far-reaching examples of interprofessional partnership integrated throughout qualifying programmes are where students from different professional programmes learn together, as illustrated in the Practice Survey. Echoing messages from the much broader CAIPE (Centre for the Advancement of Interprofessional Education) systematic reviews of interprofessional education (Barr and Waterton, 1996a, 1996b), the complexities of providing joint programmes are highlighted; however, none of the joint programmes involving qualifying social work have been rigorously evaluated. Thoroughgoing integration of partnership with users and carers within the structures, processes and content of programmes is relatively less developed, but there are some impressive examples, including the new degree programmes at the Universities of Plymouth and Dundee (Ager et al, 2005; Elliott et al, 2005).

The Practice Survey revealed an assumption that students learn about partnership in practice; yet paradoxically there is also a view among many interviewed that partnership may not be common in practice, particularly in the statutory sector. In practice learning, no examples of a defined 'partnership curriculum' were identified. The Practice Survey findings on partnership in practice learning are contradictory and frequently appear to depend on the commitment of individual organisations and practitioners. Some participants argue that practice is the 'driver' for partnership education since policy requires joint working and service user involvement. Others feel that the academic curriculum is determining the quality of partnership learning and practice is following behind.

Several studies in the Research Review (for example, Jackson and Morris, 1994) identify practice placements as a better opportunity for learning about partnership than taught modules. The process of setting up the placement was seen as an opportunity to model partnership between the student, tutor and practice teacher, but students noted the power differentials that sometimes limited their involvement.

There are an increasing number of examples in the literature of user and carer participation in teaching about partnership work, either, to use Manthorpe's (2000) distinction, as co-trainers, or as bearers of the testimony of their own experience. Three of the data extracted studies evaluate specific examples, one involving parents of children with disability (Wikler, 1979), the others, users of mental health services (Shor and Sykes, 2002; Scheyett and Kim, 2004). They suggest that a model of consumer-partnered social work education using structured dialogue acknowledges the wisdom and experience of service users, and enables them to become fully engaged in teaching, assessment, course review and curriculum committees that will shape future social workers.

Several papers make the case for user involvement in the assessment of student practice, arguing that this empowers users and carers and can provide a valuable source of feedback for students. This requires time and resources, attention to confidentiality and representation, avoidance of tokenism, and the ability to disaggregate service issues from student practice. The Research Review identified several innovative initiatives involving users and carers in student assessment, some of which were explored in the Practice Survey. However, although there are exceptions primarily in practice learning, the Practice Survey indicated that partnership work with users and carers in assessment is under-developed.

Several educators interviewed in the Practice Survey identify similarities between education for partnership and education for anti-oppressive practice (AOP). This is expressed in a number of ways: AOP is the core of effective partnership working, partnership is about managing power, it requires constant attention and is always 'work in progress'. It is also raised as a concern that partnership with users and carers is vulnerable to charges of political correctness, similar to AOP in the Diploma in Social Work (DipSW). The Research Review found that coverage of the implications of 'race', class, sexuality, religion, culture and language is not prominent in the partnership education literature. Jackson and Morris (1994) report that 'race' and language were better addressed than the potential grounds for discrimination; they argue that if there is little explicit teaching in all these areas, an understanding of how oppression can create barriers to partnership working will not be grasped.

When does education for partnership happen? The timing of interprofessional partnership learning is contested, with the issue linked to concerns about the establishment and consolidation of professional identity and confidence. Glen (2001) advocates for interprofessional learning before boundaries and stereotypes have become entrenched, but she and others (for example, Johnson, 2003) warn against the dilution of professional identity and skills where an interprofessional priority is adopted early. Kane (1976) suggested that the key was to combine understandings but contribute separate talents, and many studies conclude that it is less about *when* it happens and more about the tensions created to *fit it all in*.

In the Practice Survey, time was found to be an important aspect of developing effective partnership education. This includes both the time involved in developing and maintaining relationships and also the timing of teaching and learning about partnership. Unlike the debate about the timing of interprofessional education, also voiced in the Practice Survey, there is agreement that service user and carer involvement should begin as early as possible both in programme planning and delivery.

Who benefits from education about partnership? Where reports claim that partnership learning benefits students, they do so mainly in terms of students' attitudes and understandings, indicative of fitness to practice, rather than demonstrable practice itself. Even here, despite some positive findings (Fineberg et al, 2004; Scheyett and Diehl, 2004) some studies give a more mixed picture of the impact of partnership education on student attitudes (Shor and Sykes, 2002; Johnson, 2003; Colarossi and Forgey, 2006; Pollard et al, 2006: forthcoming). Where authors claim that the benefits of partnership learning are demonstrated in practice, it is largely in terms of skills. Students experiencing interprofessional partnership education are said to demonstrate improved collaborative, communication, conflict resolution and networking skills (for example, Alsop and Vigars, 1996). In terms of education for partnership with users and carers, students are said to improve their skills in listening, showing empathy and respect and recognising the strengths and wisdom that users and carers bring to the relationship (for example, Scheyett and

Kim, 2004). Rarely do authors claim to establish links between service outcomes for consumers, and student learning about partnership work. Consultants, users and carers warn about the pitfalls of tokenism, and 'consultationitis', whereby they are invited to participate often but too late, or too minimally to make an impact. Provided these pitfalls are avoided, there is evidence to support an increase in service user and carer contributions to social work education. Students interviewed in the Practice Survey are clear that they feel they have benefited from learning about partnership. Users and carers talk about gaining an increase in attributes such as confidence and self-esteem. In at least three programmes included in the study, they can also now gain academic credit for their participation.

Reflections on the research methodology

Shortcomings of the methodology used in the Research Review and Practice Survey should be acknowledged.

There are some limits to the overall weight to be given to some of the data extracted studies (one of the 13 studies received an overall rating of 'high', two were rated 'low' and the rest 'medium'). Six rely on single sources of data, which limits the trust that might be attributed to their findings. Their relevance to our review question, and trustworthiness, is also compromised for various reasons. Most measure changes in attitudes without follow-up into practice, yet these are not necessarily indicative of subsequent behaviour. The studies on interprofessional education favour health over other professional groups, and the number of social workers in those studies employing multiprofessional samples is very low, making it difficult to extrapolate broader findings to social workers in particular.

This is the first time that the EPPI-Centre systematic review methodology has been used in social work. The methodology has clear advantages, allowing mapping and data extraction across the full range of research methodologies. On the basis of this experience, it might be helpful to complement the systematic approach to assessing empirical methodology by developing equally rigorous scrutiny of conceptual and descriptive content.

The Practice Survey examined rather than evaluated current practice. The data from programme handbooks proved very mixed, and although it served to demonstrate that 'partnership' as a theme is largely invisible, it was not useful in mapping the territory. In contrast, the examination of module handbooks, particularly in conjunction with telephone interviews with module convenors, was a rich source of data. Similarly focus groups provided rich data.

The research team was interdisciplinary, including academics from three different disciplines, a practitioner-researcher and an early career research assistant. The team worked effectively in partnership, assisted by being co-located and having a core of prior established working relationships. The strategy to involve users, carers and students as co-researchers informed research team practice. The partnership with the EPPI-Centre proved a good source of learning.

Introduction

The essence of partnership is sharing. It is marked by respect for one another, role divisions, rights to information, accountability, competence, and value accorded to individual input. In short, each partner is seen as having something to contribute, power is shared, decisions are made jointly and roles are not only respected but are also backed by legal and moral rights.
(Tunnard, 1991, cited in Jackson and Morris, 1994, p 1)

… the notion of partnership may be more of an aspirational value than a statement of the actual nature of relationships between social workers and service users.
(Shardlow, 2000, p 259)

[Collaboration is] an unnatural act between non-consenting adults.
(interprofessional education project participant, quoted in Powell et al, 1999)

Invited in 1990 to write about her new vision of 'social work education in the year 2000' Phyllida Parsloe suggested that it should have three main concerns: partnership, poverty and peace. Her discussion focuses primarily on partnership, which she viewed as linked to an educational philosophy and structure that would support adult learning, including the opportunity to learn about partnership with others. She emphasised the importance of 'natural justice and openness', and clarity about where power and responsibility lay to assist students to experience a partnership with staff.

Parsloe suggested that partnership with service users challenges 'clientism', the devaluing of a group of people by those with power, and that if social workers are confident, clear of their role, know what they are meant to be doing, and are supported by their organisation, they are less likely to suffer the burn-out that leads to clientism.

> Above all they [social workers] need to know how to keep for themselves the discretionary space in which to develop a relationship of partnership with users within the constraints and supports of bureaucracy.
> *(Parsloe, 1990, p 18)*

She anticipated that partnership would become more likely with the development of user groups and yet paradoxically harder to achieve, as social workers are likely to feel threatened and withdraw into bureaucracy and professionalism.

Parsloe also anticipated that partnership with other professionals would be problematic because the theoretical base for this work is 'particularly meagre' (1990, p 19). Social scientists have taught with a client focus and have failed to theorise partnership with other professionals. Social work methods for work with other professionals have not developed:

> All too often, exhortation substitutes for methods and social workers are encouraged to co-operate.
> *(Parsloe, 1990, p 19)*

In 1990 Parsloe touched on the themes that 15 years later recur throughout this Review.

1.1 Regulatory context of partnership

An analysis of the regulatory context that underpins the social work degrees introduced in England, Wales, Northern Ireland and Scotland between 2003-05 indicates the following requirements for the learning, teaching and assessment of 'partnership work'.

United Kingdom
Code of Practice for Social Care Workers (2002): partnership is mentioned specifically in relation to: 'Working and respecting the roles and expertise of workers from other agencies and working in partnership with them' (6:7) and implied in terms of collaboration with service users and carers.

Quality Assurance Authority (QAA) Benchmark Statement for Social Work (1999): partnership is related to requirements such as interdisciplinary and cross-professional collaboration and engagement with service users, carers and other stakeholders. It is referred to specifically in the context of effective interagency collaboration.

National Occupational Standards (NOS) for Social Work: the concept of partnership is embedded rather than used explicitly. It is implied in ideas about collaborative working with individuals, families, carers, groups and communities, in working to develop and maintain effective working relationships and working within multidisciplinary and multiorganisational teams.

England
Department of Health Requirements for Social Work Training (2002): 'All social workers will learn and be assessed on partnership working (p 16).

Wales
Raising Standards: The Qualification Framework for the Degree in Social Work in Wales (2003), Appendix: All Wales Framework for Assessment in a Social Work Degree: based on the NOS and the QAA *Benchmark Statement*, the *Framework* refers to partnership both in terms of the development and demonstration of skills and knowledge and is implied throughout. For example: Level 1 and 2 students are required to demonstrate knowledge of interrelationships between social services and other agencies.

Northern Ireland
Northern Ireland Framework Specification for the Degree in Social Work (2003): NOS are adapted to respond to the Northern Ireland context. Partnership is mentioned both in relation to requirements during the degree and at the point of qualification. For example: knowledge of interprofessional working, working in partnership with colleagues and provider organisations and reviewing in partnership with service users. Partnership working can be inferred from other material throughout the *Framework*.

Scotland

The Framework for Social Work Education in Scotland, Standards in Social Work Education (2003): partnership is specifically mentioned throughout the *Framework* in terms of underpinning knowledge, transferable skills and competence. For example, working in partnership with service users, carers, partner organisations and colleagues in other organisations. Students must understand factors leading to effective interprofessional working. The whole of Standard 6 involves working in partnership to help individuals achieve and maintain greater independence.

1.2 Research objectives

The following objectives were stated in the proposal that resulted in the commissioning of this Knowledge Review.

- Clarify the discourse of partnership, cooperative, collaborative, multidisciplinary, interdisciplinary and interprofessional practice.
- Identify the evidence and best practice in working in partnership in all categories of social work practice and with the full range of service users and carers.
- Draw out the key messages, in particular aims and objectives, from the evidence and best practice in educational programmes for working in partnership at qualifying level and for beginning practice.
- Examine how key stakeholders (in particular, employers, practitioners and service users and carers) are involved alongside educators and practice assessors in order to maximise students' access to a range of perspectives on working in partnership.
- Evaluate the most effective approaches to organising teaching, methods of teaching and assessment of learning, about working in partnership practice – empowering students and service users will be a key criterion for this.
- Identify the most effective methods for distinguishing between core, specific and technical knowledge and skills and for preparing students for partnership practice.
- Evaluate the evidence on transferring learning within and between services, developing capacity for reflective practice and of the impact of evidence on practice.

- Evaluate the durability and sustainability of impact on learners and their practice and the available materials and infrastructure that support this.
- Highlight areas of good practice in England, Wales and Northern Ireland, the most robust evidence available internationally (in the English language) and areas for further research.

1.3 Critique of the objectives

The objectives are important and deserve a funded study that will enable them to be properly researched. However, in the context of this study they proved to be over-ambitious, with a number of difficulties:

Evaluation and effectiveness: the emphasis on 'evaluation' suggests that effectiveness could be determined from the Research Review or the Practice Survey. This only proved possible to a limited extent from the Research Review, given the paucity of robust evaluative data, and not at all from the Practice Survey, which examined, rather than evaluated, current practice.

Durability and sustainability: some findings from the Research Review, based on experience of social work education in the UK and wider (especially US) contexts, are helpful here. However, findings in the UK alone are inevitably limited. In England, some programmes began the new degree in 2003, including a small minority at MA postgraduate level. The new degrees did not begin in Northern Ireland or Wales until 2004.

Transferability and impact: findings here are limited. The majority of previous research focuses on impacts of teaching and learning on student attitudes to, and understandings of, partnership work, rather than their transfer into practice. Given the newness of the social work degree programmes, any commentary about the effectiveness of learning, teaching and assessment is inevitably tenuous, raising questions and highlighting areas for further study rather than reaching any conclusions.

'What we say and what we do': researchers were alert to the inevitable differences between espoused theory and theory in use (Argyris and

Schon, 1974). Evaluative data from the Research Review allows us to a limited extent to distinguish between these, but the lack of evaluative data on current programmes makes it difficult to differentiate between the two levels of practice.

Tacit knowledge: researchers were aware of the significance in professional practice of tacit knowledge (Polyani, 1967), where experienced practitioners know intuitively how to do something without being able to put that knowledge immediately into words, and therefore not necessarily readily accessible through questionnaire or interview formats. Such tacit knowledge, while it might be inferred from the Research Review, is not accessible to discovery in the inevitably limited scope of the Practice Survey.

Defining boundaries for exclusion and inclusion: in line with the commission, the research team attempted to draw clear boundaries around aspects of partnership for inclusion in and exclusion from the Research Review and the Practice Survey. A combination of clarification of SCIE (Social Care Institute for Excellence) priorities and our own preliminary research findings meant that these boundaries needed to be revisited at several stages. Our original intention was to exclude interprofessional education from the present Knowledge Review on grounds that a separate review of this was likely to be commissioned by SCIE. Originally we were also uncertain as to whether programme partnership structures should be included or not. The Knowledge Review indicated that both areas are viewed by stakeholders as central to the learning and teaching of partnership work. It became clear that both interprofessional partnership in social work education, and programme partnership structures should be included where, specifically, they were of direct relevance to the teaching, learning and assessment of partnership work as curriculum content, and/or as practice competence.

'Good practice': 'good practice' is not consistently defined and Fielding and his colleagues (2005) show that 'good practice' is a very contested concept, particularly among practitioners. Concepts of 'good practice' deployed in the Research Review may, where the evaluative data allows, be derived directly from evidence of their effectiveness, even though criteria for judging the latter are always likely to be contested. For the

Practice Survey, however, examining but not evaluating education practice, it has been necessary to develop rather different indicators of 'good practice'.

1.4 Conceptual challenges

Conceptual hybridity and confusion about 'partnership' is seemingly endemic to the topic. Discussing interprofessional partnership, Barr (1996), Whittington (2003) and Trevillion and Bedford (2003), among others, point to the ambiguous nature of 'partnership work' in social work education, with terms such as 'collaboration', 'cooperation', 'multi and interdisciplinary', 'multi and interprofessional' often used interchangeably. In this Review the term 'interprofessional' is used unless a study is cited that uses an alternative. In relation to users and carers, not only is the concept of 'partnership' taken to mean different things in different contexts, but a range of different terms, such as 'participation', 'involvement', even 'empowerment', with often different connotations, are used to describe it (Jackson and Morris, 1994; Ager et al, 2005).

To provide a structure to the Knowledge Review, and in response to the commission to examine partnership both with users and carers and between professionals, the research team had initially conceptualised partnership at four broad levels. However, in consultation with the stakeholder group, it became apparent that an additional three levels of partnership relationship must be included, despite initial agreement with SCIE about excluding the theme of interprofessional education:

1. Social work student and service user/carer
2. Social work student and educator/assessor
3. Educator/assessor and stakeholder including users/carers, employers and practitioners
4. Higher Education Institution and stakeholder
5. Social work student and student from another professional education programme
6. Social work student and social work student
7. Social work academic and academic from another discipline.

The conceptual confusion, and with it drawing boundaries for the scope of the Review, was continually challenging, and it proved essential at several stages to clarify and re-clarify the Review focus. Discussions with SCIE in the early stages of the work were helpful in this regard; they clarified that our central focus was to be on teaching, learning and assessment of partnership work, and the development of partnership practice competence. Partnership-based organisational structures were not to be included unless they focused explicitly on education about partnership work; interprofessional education was to be included only in so far as it held the same focus. Throughout, the research team needed to remain responsive and consistent in its treatment of the many and varied understandings of partnership that were articulated in research and practice.

One noteworthy difficulty concerned making the distinction between involvement of service users and carers in social work education, and a specific focus on working in partnership with them. Unlike interprofessional education, where it was easier to draw the line between, for example, shared learning among students from different disciplines about common topics, and learning about working together, the boundary was less easily drawn with users and carers. Commonly, the expressed pedagogical purpose of including service users and carers in the education process was to enable students to learn from them about their experiences, to understand them better and value them more highly. Explicitly or implicitly, this was considered to be the foundation for working in partnership with them. On balance, the Review team erred on the side of inclusivity when considering user and carer involvement, participation and partnership in social work education.

1.5 The stakeholder group

The purpose of the stakeholder group was to engage users and carers, social work practitioners and employers, and students as partners in the Knowledge Review in two different ways, as *critical friends* at key stages in the Knowledge Review and as *researchers* in the Practice Survey.

Stakeholder group membership

Users' and carers' representatives from: CAPITAL, a West Sussex group of paid and voluntary members who have experience of using mental health services; the Brighton and Hove Somali Elders Group; and ESDA, the East Sussex Disability Association. At an early meeting, the stakeholder group expressed a view that it might be useful to engage a group of young service users to interview students; however, in the limited time available for the research, it proved unrealistic to establish a relationship with the relevant group and then invite them to participate.

Students: two BA Social Work (University of Sussex and University of Brighton), and two MA Social Work (University of Sussex).

Practitioner representatives: Voice of the Child; West Sussex Council Residential Centre for Children with Disabilities; and independent Long Arm Practice Teacher.

Employer representatives: Training and Development Officers from East Sussex and Brighton and Hove Councils.

Stakeholder activities

As *critical friends* the intention was to engage stakeholders at key stages in the work of the Review. The pace of work and the short time-scale meant that it was not possible to fully involve stakeholders in all key research decisions. However, during the four formal meetings of the stakeholder group, members commented on:

- the composition and brief of the stakeholder group
- the process of the Review
- the review question
- the criteria for good practice
- the telephone and focus group questionnaires used in the Practice Survey
- the draft Final Report.

As *researchers*, the aim was to engage stakeholders primarily as members of the Practice Survey focus group research teams. This was initially conceptualised as engaging users and carers as researchers (Joseph Rowntree Foundation, 2005), but the first meeting of the stakeholder group was pivotal in a decision to invite students to participate alongside academic researchers and users and carers in leading the focus groups. As a result, users and carers and students were each involved as researchers in three site visits. This provided an unexpected but extensive opportunity for informal 'consultation' during the process of preparation for and operation of the focus groups. Furthermore, working to achieve partnership with users and carers and students during the study proved a significant source of learning for the academic researchers. One immediate outcome was a letter to the university finance office setting out issues in relation to payment to service users and carers as researchers. One member of the stakeholder group, with suitable academic qualifications, received training from the research team in the EPPI-Centre keywording methods, and made valuable contributions to data collection for the Research Review as well.

2

Research Review

2.1 Methodology

2.1.1 Background and review question

SCIE evaluative reviews are designed to locate, as far as possible, all relevant material, to evaluate the strength of evidence and to make recommendations for policy and practice. Sources beyond empirical work, such as commentaries, theoretical contributions, narrative accounts, policy documents and inspection evidence are drawn on to contextualise the findings, but data extraction and detailed quality judgements are applied to empirical work only.

In refining the inclusion and exclusion criteria below, we initially identified three possible foci for the partnerships – *competence* in partnership work, *content focus* on partnership work in curricula and *organisation* of education that involves partnerships. As discussed in section 1.4, further discussion with SCIE clarified that both partnership-based organisation and inteprofessional education were included only where they had a direct bearing on education and competence in partnership work.

The review question thus became:

What do we know about the teaching, learning and assessment of partnership work in social work education?

The Research Review team undertook training with the EPPI-Centre in relation to all stages of the systematic reviewing process. Additionally, all stages of the reviewing process were quality assured by a designated EPPI-Centre representative.

2.1.2 Searching

The full Search Strategy (26 pages) is available as an online appendix at the following address: www.scie.org.uk/publications/knowledgereviews/kr10appendix.pdf

The search strategy covered the following types of sources:

- empirical studies from peer-reviewed sources
- research papers from non-peer-reviewed sources
- professional and policy documents
- other relevant published/unpublished literature
- theoretical papers from peer-reviewed sources (to inform the framework for synthesis).

The full details of the search strategy and databases used are given in Appendix 1. In total, 4,654 citations were yielded (including duplicates).

2.1.3 Inclusion and exclusion criteria

All studies identified through the search strategy were screened according to agreed inclusion and exclusion criteria, refined during the early stages of the Review. The criteria were:

- qualifying not post-qualifying education and training;
- training and education: any activity explicitly intended to contribute to the qualifying process, in whatever context it took place;
- social work: studies were included that focus on social workers or include them as part of a multiprofessional focus;
- focus on partnership in curriculum content and/or practice competence (see section 1.4);
- interprofessional education, focused on inteprofessional partnership work;
- studies in the English language: it was acknowledged that there was likely to be some important and interesting work being reported in other languages, but there was not the scope to review these.

No limits were placed on the date of publication, as it was agreed that there may be a small number of early studies that had a profound effect on later developments.

Studies which focused on any of the aspects of partnership outlined in section 1.4 were included, although those focusing on practice competence were only included where the study was in the context of social work education, and not where the focus was on competence in front-line practice.

Preliminary application of the inclusion criteria (before refinement) yielded 638 citations (including duplicates). Refinement and narrowing of the criteria, as discussed, reduced the number of unique citations to 260 (that is, excluding duplicates) to be included in the Research Review. It was not possible to obtain full copies of 25 of these cited works. Final application of the refined inclusion criteria was done on reading in full each of the 235 cited works obtained; this yielded 119 publications, 117 of them published and 2 in press (no other unpublished material). In some cases, several publications discussed the same study. In all, there were 109 separate studies included in the Research Review (see Appendix 1 for details).

2.1.4 Keywording

The 109 studies meeting the inclusion criteria are referred to henceforth as 'studies included in the Review'. All were keyworded, using a system revised from the existing EPPI-Centre keywording system, which had been designed for reviews of education research literature, and did not adequately cover social work concepts, partnership or social work education practices. The revised keywording system, as shown in Appendix 2, was designed to code key attributes of each study, including, for example, the status and location of the study, the type and level of partnership work considered, the focus on academic or practice learning, and the presence or absence of an empirical base. Seventeen per cent were double keyworded and moderation sessions held to establish inter-rater reliability and a further 10% went to the EPPI-Centre team representative for quality assurance.

2.1.5 In-depth review

In line with the EPPI-Centre principles and practice, data extraction was designed to be used across the full range of research methodologies. A map of the research, based on all studies included in the Review, was discussed with SCIE and the stakeholder group prior to making the final selection of studies for data extraction. The process of final selection of the studies for data extraction involved applying the additional criterion that the study was sufficiently empirical, and the methodology sufficiently reported, to be able to be subjected to data extraction. The criteria relating to partnership work and interprofessional education were applied more stringently at this stage; since, unlike the other inclusion criteria, these were more open to interpretation. Each study was data extracted by two team members. Data extraction included rigorous judgements of validity, reliability, user engagement and quality of the research design, execution and reporting. Additionally, the EPPI-Centre team member linked to the Review quality assured three of the 13 data extracted studies.

2.1.6 Synthesis of the data

The studies did not yield sufficient quantitative data to undertake any statistical analyses.

Synthesis of data was undertaken according to the question or subquestions that they address, and to themes that emerged from the findings and conclusions drawn in the studies. These themes do not correspond directly with the coding categories established in the early stages of the project to provide schema for keywording included studies (see Appendix 2). Rather, they were elicited through scrutiny of the information gleaned from each study as a product of the keywording process, and in dialogue with members of the Practice Survey research team, and the stakeholder group. Our purpose was to elicit cross-cutting themes relevant to and informative for synthesising data from both the Research and the Practice Survey components of the Review. Once the potential themes had been identified, all studies included in the Research Review were revisited, testing and confirming the relevance and validity of the themes for synthesising the research data gathered.

Accordingly, findings from both the Research Review and the Practice Survey are organised under the following thematic headings:

- What do we mean by partnership in social work education?
- Why is partnership important in social work education?
- Who does partnership in social work education involve?
- What does partnership in social work education include, and how is it included?
- When does partnership education happen?
- Who benefits from education about partnership?

2.2 Overview of the literature

2.2.1 Introduction

The 109 studies included in the Research Review were predominantly from the UK or US, and range from 1972 to those currently in press (see Table 1). They explore the question of partnership work in social work education from a wide range of perspectives, drawing on specific educational programmes, on reviews or surveys of wider educational provision, or simply on reflections on the existing literature and practice experience. The majority take as their focus education about interprofessional partnership work, but a significant minority address partnership work with users and carers, and some deal with both. Almost twice as many concentrate on classroom learning as on practice learning.

Thirteen studies meeting the inclusion criteria were included for detailed data extraction in this Review. Alongside these, however, were a further 12, which might have been worthy of data extraction had time and resources allowed. Three of these discuss partnership work with service users and carers (Cuming and Wilkins, 2000; Pierpont et al, 2001; Elliott et al, 2005); one concerns partnership between educators and students (Huff and Johnson, 1998), with the remainder focusing on interprofessional partnership work (Chartier et al, 1984; Tope, 1995; Etchells et al, 1999; Sims, 1999; Simoni, 2000; Maidenburg and Golick, 2001; Flaherty et al, 2003; Grossman and McCormick, 2003). All of these studies receive attention in the 'in-depth' component of the Research Review (section 2.3).

A further 16 studies make some reference to empirical evidence, but were not considered eligible for in-depth quality assessment. Most commonly (12 cases), they make reference to student or user feedback or course evaluation information, but offer little or no methodological detail. In addition, five studies focus on interprofessional education, but with insufficient emphasis on partnership work or qualifying social work education to merit in-depth scrutiny. Noteworthy examples are both a UK survey and a systematic review of interprofessional education in health and social care, conducted by CAIPE (Barr, 1996; Barr and Waterton, 1996a, 1996b; Hammick, 2000; Koppel et al, 2001). These yield a range of informative findings. Since, however, they do not pay discrete attention either to qualifying level or to social work education,

Table 1
Overview of all included studies

Studies	Number
UK	52
USA	48
Other (European, Canadian, Australian)	9
Focus on partnership with users and carers	41
Focus on partnership between students and educators	23
Focus on interprofessional partnership	81
Focus on classroom curriculum	107
Focus on practice learning	64
Some empirical base (not data extracted)	28
Data extracted	13

nor to partnership work as opposed to broader interprofessional learning, it was not appropriate to include them for data extraction in this Review.

It is essential to clarify from the outset that the 'in-depth review' that follows, although inclusive of messages from the 13 data extracted studies, provides an integration of the findings and arguments of all studies included in the Research Review. A majority of the papers included have little or no empirical research base. They describe or review existing provision, and/or reflect on the basis of previous evidence, experience and values. Since most of these were not, therefore, subjected to detailed quality and relevance assessment, their findings may be taken to inform consideration of our review question, but must be treated throughout as suggestive or indicative only.

In the interests of providing a clear, informative but relatively succinct overview of the literature, when mapping the broad research field (as distinct from the 13 studies considered in detail), we focus our attention rather more on work addressing partnership with users and carers, and to some extent partnership between students and educators, than on interprofessional partnership. This does not reflect the balance of the literature, where focus on education for interprofessional partnership work featured prominently (see Table 1). However, our emphasis was chosen in the light both of the original brief from SCIE, and the likelihood that a separate review of interprofessional education will be commissioned. We chose to given particular attention in the overview to some of the most recent UK-based work expressly considering the new social work qualifying degree.

Also, in the interests of clarity and accessibility, where discussion points are commonly raised in the literature, we provide indicative but not exhaustive references. Where distinctive arguments are made, initiatives described, or findings presented, we discuss these specifically.

2.2.2 What do we mean by partnership in social work education?

A hybrid, contested and taken-for-granted concept

In the context of social work education, as in practice, the concept of 'partnership' work is loosely defined, expressed through multiple terminologies, embodying different nuances, at one and the same time both contested and taken for granted (Parsloe, 1990; Jackson and Morris, 1994). From the outset of the Review, this alone presented significant challenges in defining the boundaries for exploring our sources. Our aim here is to try to encapsulate the primary constructs used in the literature denoting what may broadly be considered to be 'partnership work' in social work education.

Noteworthy is the variety of discourses used to describe what we will call 'partnership work' in the content, processes or outcomes of social work education. 'Partnership' itself is a term fairly commonly used in the UK literature, much less so in North America and elsewhere. There is a plethora of other terms to be grappled with: participation and participatory action, involvement and collaboration, as well as interprofessional, interdisciplinary, multiprofessional, shared, or joint education/practice, to name but a few. Only a minority of papers explicitly attempt to define what they mean. On the positive side, this hybridity alone allows the space for many and varied initiatives in social work education. More negatively, however, neither the hybridity nor the potential tensions embedded within the concept of partnership itself receive much, if any, attention within the social work education literature. Noteworthy by its absence, for example, is any significant discussion of the complexities of working in partnership with service users for whom intervention is unwelcome and/or resisted.

Levels of partnership work

Ager and colleagues (2005), discussing both the social work degree programme at the University of Dundee, and an earlier audit of eight social work programmes in Scotland, draw on an adaptation by Mackay (2002) of Arnstein's 'ladder of participation'. The adaptation was designed with reference to user participation in practice, but may easily be applied to the education context. It identifies 'levels' of participation along the continuum: not involved, informed, consulted, attended working groups, influence on action, shared action, delegated function, controlled decisions and actions. While best not applied in too rigid or linear a fashion, the model can be illuminative in judging what is meant by partnership, in the content and the processes or outcomes of social work education.

Much of the literature describes partnership work that is effectively at the lower end of the continuum, including, typically, consultation with users and carers and their involvement in academic or practice-based curricula. Users and carers are, for example, invited to bring their own testimonies, share their experiences or act as trainers with students in the classroom (Pickering and Mullender, 1991; Curran, 1997; Brandon and Knapp, 1999; Boylan et al, 2000; Scheyett and Kim, 2004), to engage with student learning in the community (Morrison et al, 1997; Brandon and Knapp, 1999; Hendricks and Rudich, 2000), or informally to provide feedback on student practice (Wikler, 1979; Cuming and Wilkins, 2000; Edwards, 2003; Elliott et al, 2005).

In some contexts, however, the meaning of partnership is extended considerably further along Mackay's continuum, to embrace some degree of shared action and influence on outcomes. Among other writers articulating this approach (Scheyett and Diehl, 2004; Ager et al, 2005; Elliott et al, 2005), Curran (1997) has described the establishment of 'collective workshops' on the (old) Diploma in Social Work (DipSW) programme at the University of Bath. The workshops integrated users and carers with educators, practitioners and advocates, at all levels of planning, providing and reviewing teaching in mental health.

Teamwork, collaborative practice and group work

The hybridity of concepts related to 'partnership work' in the literature is partly accounted for by the range of underpinning theorisations of professional practice and role. Some authors frame their discussions in the language of teamwork and collaboration. Partnership in this sense is about the development of cooperative learning as team members (Bordelon, 2003), of communication, cooperation and coordination either between professionals or between practitioners and users (Jivanjee and Friesen, 1997; Brandon and Knapp, 1999; Lough et al, 1999; Patford, 2001; Flaherty et al, 2003). Alongside this is a particular focus on understandings and negotiations of professional roles, remits and identities, complementarities and differences (Tendler and Metzger, 1978; Alsop and Vigars, 1996; Barr, 1996).

A few authors draw on theories of group work underpinning partnership-oriented initiatives in social work education. Kacen (1998) provides an interesting example of an exercise in 'intergroup bridging', grounded in existentialist, gestalt and learning theories, to increase understandings and reduce potential tensions between the student, professional and user.

Partnership as empowerment, as ideal and reality

For some writers, partnership is the expression of a core social work value, with concepts of rights, exclusion, discrimination and power central to the thrust of participatory practice (Jackson and Morris, 1994; Curran, 1997; Boylan et al, 2000). Discussing both the process and the content of social work education, Curran (1997) identifies four dimensions of power to be challenged: power in observable decision making, in non-observable decision making, in the construction and defining of concepts, and through the discursive practices linking power to knowledge. She contends that partnership must be embedded throughout social work education – 'a whole-programme philosophy' – with the lived experience of users, carers and students foregrounded, and the knowledge and status of 'experts' challenged at all times.

Not unrelated to this are some interesting debates about whether partnership denotes an ideal, an 'aspiration' (Shardlow, 2000), or a reality. Trevillion and Bedford (2003) make the distinction between the objectives of 'pragmatism', whereby students learn how to work together with other professionals in the real external world, and 'utopianism', whereby they learn to become flexible, holistic practitioners – interprofessional selves, for a better future world. In contrast, Curran, discussing partnership with users and carers, rejects exactly such a distinction as a 'form of repressive power':

> User empowerment was not promoted to deny reality, but as recognition of users' lived experiences.
> *(Curran, 1997, pp 31-2)*

2.2.3 Why is partnership work important in social work education?

'A formidable mandate'

Ager et al (2005) express the view of many authors, that in the 21st century we have a 'formidable mandate' to involve users and carers in social work services, and that those involved in social work education have a responsibility to carry through this mandate. Ager et al describe user and carer involvement in social work education as a slowly emerging process, linked to social trends such as the consumerism of the 1980s, the development of social models of disability and disability rights movements, public unease about poverty and social exclusion, and the lack of accountability of welfare services. More recently, emancipatory legislation surrounding human rights, and user and carer rights in particular, 'has raised the question of why the consumers of social work services are not much more keenly involved in educating and assessing social workers' (Ager et al, 2005, p 468).

Policy and practice imperatives

A majority of writers arguing the education case either for partnership with users and carers or between professionals, locate their work within contemporary policy contexts. In the UK and elsewhere, they draw attention towards the requirements for, and moves towards, both 'joined-up' services across professional domains, and services that are inclusive of and responsive to the voices of users and carers (Jivanjee and Friesen,

1997; Brandon and Knapp, 1999; Connolly and Novak, 2000; Ager et al, 2005). These imperatives demand not only organisational restructuring, but the re-alignment of professional orientation, understandings and skills. They define and shape the world of practice for which we are preparing social work students.

More specifically, the requirement for qualifying social work pro-grammes to embrace partnership work has been formalised in education policy and guidance in both the UK and the US, providing an explicit rationale for addressing the issue. Humphris and Hean (2004) argue that the emphasis on interprofessional learning is driven by government policy to improve the quality of collaboration against a background of failures in interprofessional systems. In the UK context, Elliott et al (2005) are among the first to give a full account of the development of the new degree at the University of Plymouth, expressly designed to pro-mote user and carer involvement in line with the government initiatives outlined in the Department of Health *Quality Strategy for Social Care* (2000). Ager et al (2005) discuss similar developments in the Scottish context, at the University of Dundee.

Social work value base and empowerment

For a distinct constituency of educators and authors, the commitment to partnership work in social work education is grounded not just in policy requirements, but in a philosophy and value base central to the core of social work. For Parsloe (1990) and Parsloe and Swift (1997), educating for partnership work is about upholding standards of natural justice all too easily submerged under bureaucracy, and challenging the 'client-ism' that devalues the powerless. Hendricks and Rudich (2000) make a different but related point, when championing the case for involving students in collaborative 'community building'. They cite social work's history of service to communities, by way of challenge to individualised and agency-specific intervention.

Probably the strongest value-based manifesto for partnership in social work education comes from those who place partnership and/or participation within the discourses of rights and power, with strong commitment to empowerment, often alongside anti-discriminatory or AOP (Jackson and Morris, 1994; Curran, 1997; Boylan et al, 2000; Scheyett and Diehl, 2004). Scheyett and Diehl argue passionately that partnership and empowerment should also be at the core of social work education content and processes:

> Can we truly teach social work values of self-determination, partnership and empowerment within an educational system that does not model and operationalize these values and its own processes?
> *(Scheyett and Diehl, 2004, p 436)*

Because it works?

The final rationale most commonly given for educating social work students in partnership work, both states the obvious and begs questions. Taking the obvious first, most papers seek to substantiate their cases by citing research evidence demonstrating that partnership 'works' in practice. Hence it is worth educating our social workers to be effective partnership-oriented practitioners since, it is claimed, we know that partnership improves the quality of experience and outcomes for users and carers alike (Beresford, 1994; Brandon and Knapp, 1999; Pierpont et al, 2001; Gonzales et al, 2004; Elliott et al, 2005). Likewise, the argument is put that we know from experience how much more effective are services and practices that are collaborative, integrated and/or inter-professional, than those that are not (Burns et al, 2000; Patford, 2001; Damon-Rodriguez and Corley, 2002; Humphris and Hean, 2004).

More open to question is the rationale for partnership education in social work based on the claim that it 'works', improving the quality of students as practitioners-to-be (Curran, 1997; Huff and Johnson, 1998; Brandon and Knapp, 1999; Connolly and Novak, 2000; Cuming and Wilkins, 2000; Pierpont et al, 2001; Bordelon, 2003; Tew et al, 2003), and for users or carers (Curran, 1997; Jivanjee and Friesen, 1997; Boylan et al, 2000; Connolly and Novak; 2000, Cuming and Wilkins, 2000; Tew et al, 2003; Scheyett and Kim, 2004; Elliott et al, 2005). Glen (2001), for example, notes the limited empirical base for the widely held view that interprofessional education 'adds value' by paving the way to collaborative practice. On the basis of preliminary evidence, she concludes that the picture is likely to be more complex: different interprofessional educational structures are likely to lead to different outcomes. More broadly, the findings of this Research Review confirm that there is a need for caution in asserting that partnership education 'works'. Many of the studies making such claims are not amenable to in-depth scrutiny; those that are may still leave some questions for the transfer of learning into professional practice and identity.

2.2.4 Who does partnership in social work education involve?

As outlined in the introduction to this Knowledge Review, our original proposal envisaged four 'levels' of partnership relationships, with three more subsequently added.

Many papers make reference to the several partnership relationships commonly involved in education processes and organisation, curriculum content and associated practice competences. Russell and Hymans (1999), for example, discussing an interprofessional community-based project, identify a content and practice competence focus on partnership between social work and nursing students, and between students and users. The process and organisation of this practice learning experience involved partnership between all of these stakeholders, as well as between nursing and social work educators, and between the educators and community organisations. Not least, such examples demonstrate the complexity of what was often involved.

Most reported interprofessional partnership education involves health-related professions – nursing primarily, as well as occupational therapy, speech therapy, midwifery and general practice, and, less commonly, law and education (Sklar, and Torczyner, 1991; Tope, 1996; Simoni, 2000; Maidenburg and Golick, 2001). The range of users and carers involved is wide, with, among others, examples from mental health social work (Hewstone et al, 1994; Powell et al, 1999; Pierpont et al, 2001; Karban, 2003), disability (Chartier et al, 1984; Etchells and Kniveton, 2000; Johnston and Banks, 2000; Maidenburg and Golick, 2001; Sable et al, 2001), child and family support (Brandon and Knapp, 1999; Tracy and Pine, 2000; Miller et al, 2001; Grossman and McCormick, 2003) and child protection (Jackson and Morris, 1994; Hendricks and Rudich, 2000; Tucker, 2003). Interestingly, there appears to be no less attention paid to partnership with users and carers in areas of practice that may involve some degree of social control – such as mental health and child protection – than in others. As discussed earlier, the potential for partnership work with involuntary clients appears taken somewhat for granted, rather than problematised in itself as a topic for critical reflection in social work education.

Notable by its absence is any significant discussion of working in partnership either with user and carer organisations or with other professional organisations, as opposed to their representatives. Many studies describe partnership arrangements made with professional agencies or user and carer groups in order to facilitate partnership education initiatives (for example, Chartier et al, 1984; Maidenburg and Golick, 2001; Shor and Sykes, 2002; Torkington et al, 2002, 2003, 2004). Several emphasise the significance of understanding organisational cultures in order to achieve effective interprofessional work (Barr and Waterton, 1996a, 1996b; Glen, 2001; Pollard et al, 2006: forthcoming). However, few expressly discuss student learning to work with other organisations, rather than other people, as the focus of curriculum content or practice competence.

2.2.5 What does partnership in social work education include, and how is it included?

Partnership as embedded in social work education

One of the most salient issues for those planning social work education is the question of where and how partnership work sits, both within curricula, and within programme structures and processes. By far the majority of the initiatives reported to date concern discrete courses or practice learning projects, many of them demonstrating the 'creative and inclusive methods of promoting partnership' called for by Levin (2004) on behalf of SCIE. From these, there runs a continuum through more comprehensive partnership-oriented developments, to (more rarely) wholesale integration of partnership, in partnership.

The most far-reaching examples of embedded interprofessional partnership initiatives reported are those where a dual qualifying programme was established, training 'joint practitioners' or 'hybrid workers'. We found reports of three such programmes in England. (It is worth noting that these were prior to the introduction of the new degree framework, which allows for shared learning but not dual qualification.) At London South Bank University students trained together for a joint social work and nursing degree in learning disabilities (Sims, 1999; Trevillion and

Bedford, 2003). The same specialism was involved in the former joint DipSW/DipHE (Nursing) programme at the Universities of Salford and Manchester (Etchells et al, 1999; Etchells and Kniveton, 2000). At Portsmouth in the mid-1990s nursing and social work students learned together, apparently to become 'twice the practitioner' in mental health (McCray, 1995). In North America, we found two initiatives of this sort reported. The first was an early joint Masters programme in social work (MSW) and public health at the University of Minnesota (McClelland, 1985); the second, a joint qualifying degree in law and social work, at McGill University in Canada (Sklar and Torczyner, 1991). Echoing messages from the wide-ranging CAIPE systematic review of interprofessional education in health and social care (Barr and Waterton, 1996a, 1996b), all five reports highlight the many complexities of providing joint programmes. Unfortunately, none of these initiatives appears to have been evaluated systematically. This said, all of the authors are positive about their achievements and the potential for student learning.

The case for fundamental integration of partnership with users and carers into the structures and processes of social work education programmes, and at a level that might equate with the middle or higher rungs of Mackay's ladder (Mackay, 2002, cited in Ager et al, 2005), has some strong protagonists. As Scheyett and Diehl assert:

> … [in] a true partnership between clients and social workers in social work education.… Clients would have significant roles throughout the educational process, working together with educators in establishing goals for social work education, creating strategies to meet these goals, and implementing and evaluating these educational strategies in formal academic settings.
> *(Scheyett and Diehl, 2004, p 436)*

As yet, there are few, if any, manifestations of this ideal reported in the literature. Ager et al (2005), discussing their 2004 audit of qualifying social work programmes in Scotland, found (with some exception at the Open University) very little evidence of user and carer involvement in the governance of education programmes. Closest perhaps comes the model of the Service User and Carer Group involved in the new social work degree at the University of Dundee. This stakeholder group, linked to a grassroots network of local user and carer groups, has formal representation within programme structures, meets regularly, and has been involved from the outset in strategic design, development, planning, delivery and ongoing review of the degree programme. The initiative is too young yet to have been evaluated. But as reported by Ager et al, it embodies for students and carers the ethos of partnership not just in content, but modelled and made real in processes embedded throughout the programme.

Some other initiatives demonstrate similar commitment to partnership work embedded in the structures of part, if not all, of the programmes involved. There are many examples where social work students are given the opportunity to work together with other students on interprofessional modules, projects or workshops, albeit often elective rather than core. Structural barriers to these can be many; overcoming them requires clarity of purpose, commitment to cross-discipline collaboration and institutional support infrastructures (Gronski and Pigg, 2000). Among the many papers discussing such initiatives are several data extracted in this Research Review; these are more fully discussed in section 2.3 (Carpenter and Hewstone, 1996; Johnson, 2003; Fineberg et al, 2004; Colarossi and Forgey, 2006: forthcoming; Pollard et al, 2006: forthcoming).

A current example of partnership work with users and carers embedded in substantial parts (if not the whole) of the programme, is the establishment at the University of Plymouth of 'collective workshops'. These involve a consultative group of users, carers, academics and practitioners meeting regularly and working collaboratively to develop practice learning for the new degree (Elliott et al, 2005). As with the Dundee example, the emphasis here is on rejecting tokenism, embedding and modelling partnership work within programme structures and processes, as well as teaching and learning about partnership work and how to do it, within the practice setting. By way of critique of the NOS and General Social Care Council (GSCC) requirements for practice, the consultative group concluded that those 'would mean only tokenistic participation from users and carers due to their prescriptive nature'. They describe as a 'transforming moment … the first step towards real and meaningful collaboration between professionals and users and carers' the decision to start instead from the question: 'what should a student social worker look like at each stage of practice?' (Elliott et al, 2005, p 454).

Discrete initiatives for partnership work – classroom based

Far more prevalent are accounts of discrete teaching and learning initiatives within social work education programmes. These focus on partnership with users and carers, between professions, or both, and take place within the classroom and practice learning arenas.

In the classroom setting, there are a good few examples of direct user and carer participation in teaching about partnership work, either, to use Manthorpe's distinction, as co-trainers, or as bearers of the testimony of their own experience (Manthorpe, 2000). Boylan et al (2000), for example, tell us of care leavers invited to discuss, on an equal footing with DipSW students, their perceptions of social workers, and the Citizens as Trainers Group et al (2004) report empowering young citizens as social work trainers. Likewise, mental health service users and/or carers have been involved in particular modules or workshops as consumer teachers (Curran, 1997; Jivanjee and Friesen, 1997; Shor and Sykes, 2002), as have members of learning disability user groups (Pickering and Mullender, 1991). Occasionally, as with the Israeli 'intergroup bridging – dynamic circles exercise', users have also participated in structured exercises or role-play (Kacen, 1998). In another instance, carers of children with long-term neurological developmental disabilities or illness have acted as teachers and advisors to students, using a solution-based approach in collaborative and interdisciplinary working (Gonzales et al, 2004).

Several authors have been careful to draw attention to key practicalities and points of principle in managing the process of user and carer participation in social work education. Among these are: fair and realistic remuneration for participants; physical access; the need for careful planning, preparation and support of trainers; attention to relational issues and power imbalances; agreements about confidentiality; and dangers of atypical representation and of labelling participants according to their user or carer status while sidelining their identity (Manthorpe, 2000; Levin, 2004; Elliott et al, 2005).

The objectives of the classroom-based initiatives reported are, for the most part, to inform and develop students' understandings of users' and carers' experiences and views, to confound stereotypes, to learn skills in communication and inclusive behaviour, and to question their own roles and status. For users and carers, the objectives most commonly reported are to allow their voices to be heard, to be valued and understood, to make a contribution to student learning and potentially to the improved quality of professional practice.

There are some particularly distinctive classroom-based initiatives worth noting. Independently, Scheyett and Diehl (2004) and Scheyett and Kim (2004) in the US, and Shor and Sykes (2002) in Israel, describe the use of 'structured dialogue' between mental health users and social work students. Structured opportunities are created for students to hear from users about their experiences of illness, of life and of the 'helping' professions. Facilitators guide the encounters, taking responsibility for introducing themes for discussion, ensuring that the conversation flows, and that all participants have a voice. Both initiatives are described as successful. The authors conclude that there is strong potential for the structured dialogue model to improve student attitudes towards, and learning about, people with mental illness, and to undermine the one-dimensional representations and pre-existing stereotypes with which students may start out. Feedback from users and carers contributing to structured dialogue sessions indicated its validating and empowering potential for them. Less structured an approach is the 'user conversation' described by Elliot et al (2005) at the University of Plymouth. Here, users and carers meet individually with students to discuss 'what they think a good social worker should be like'. Students write an account of the conversation and users and carers give direct feedback on their interpersonal skills, the values and assumptions they display, the accuracy of their account and their ability to reflect on feedback. The process models a reversal of the usual power relationship, with users and carers also as informal assessors, judging students according to user/carer defined criteria.

There are reports of a range of classroom-based opportunities for learning about partnership work that do not involve the direct participation of users or carers, nor indeed of students from other disciplines. None is especially distinctive, and the learning methods and content themes involved fit broadly within the summary provided below.

Discrete initiatives for partnership work – practice based

Many of the practice learning opportunities privileging interprofessional partnership work that are reported in the literature take place in agency settings. Some are multidisciplinary, and most are primary health or other health-related (Tendler and Metzger, 1978; Lowry, 1987; Lough et al, 1996; Cuming and Wilkins, 2000; Cook et al, 2001; Torkington et al, 2003). The focus commonly is on students' socialisation, their developing student understanding of other professions and intergroup relations, recognition of role distinctions, boundaries and complementarity, understanding of common and different core knowledge and value bases, and the development of collaborative, communication, networking and conflict resolution skills (Barr and Waterton, 1996a, 1996b).

Several papers also give accounts of interesting community-based practice learning initiatives. The focus here is on student learning, in collaboration with community groups and outside of agency settings, about users' and carers' lives and lifestyles and their service needs. Bordelon (2003), for example, describes a 'co-operative, participatory learning project', where students worked together with a local disability community action group, framing proposals to meet their service needs, and in doing so developing their knowledge, collaborative and interpersonal skills. Unfortunately no evaluative data as such are presented, but the author reflects that outcomes exceeded expectations, in terms of 'trusting relationships' established and active participation achieved. Other North American projects also have a distinctive community action or community development focus, encouraging students to work with and learn from users as community members and as resources, rather than as victims (Morrison et al, 1997; Hendricks and Rudich, 2000).

Two papers focus on the teaching and learning of research practice as fertile ground for learning about partnership work. Julia and Kondrat's recent review of the teaching of participatory action research found it strikingly absent from MSW programmes in the US (Julia and Kondrat, 2000). However, Pierpont et al (2001) describe an innovative 'empowerment research' project, with students learning from users as experts, about the impact of policy and practice on their lives.

Teaching and learning: methods and content themes

The methods of learning and teaching deployed in social work education about partnership are many and varied. Whether or not the participants include stakeholders other than social work students and educators, there is a preponderance of adult learning methods described, involving interactive, experiential, enquiry and practice-based learning, rather than received learning (Parsloe, 1990; Barr and Waterton, 1996a, 1996b; Burns et al, 2000; Glen, 2001; Sable et al, 2001).

The content of teaching and learning centres around several key themes. Primary among these is knowledge and understanding about the experiences, identities, perspectives and value bases of others, be they users and carers or others. Alongside these, more prominently in the context of interprofessional partnership work, is an emphasis on the understanding of professional roles, their complementarity and boundaries, the potential for role conflict and the need for role clarity. Teamwork and, less commonly, group work, may provide the conceptual framework for understanding both how professionals may work together, and how they may work with users and carers. Core skills provide another central focus, with the emphasis on collaboration, communication and networking, as well as interpersonal and advocacy skills.

User and carer assessment of partnership work

Several papers make the case for user involvement in the assessment of student practice, arguing that this can empower users and carers and provide a valuable source of feedback for students (Jackson and Morris, 1994; Cuming and Wilkins, 2000; Edwards, 2003). Parsloe and Swift (1997), in a brief workshop report of their research for the Department of Health, maintain that users bring to such assessment not only their unique experience of the student's practice, but also different criteria from educators for judging practice qualities. Likewise the early work of Wikler (1979), more firmly grounded in empirical evidence, identified that while educators prioritised various aspects of student 'behaviour', carers were more concerned with 'experiential' qualities, in particular the capacity to 'really listen'. A similar point was made by the collective workshops at the University of Plymouth, in rejecting NOS criteria, in favour of their own sense of 'what a student social worker should look like' (Elliott et al, 2005).

As yet, there are few examples to be found of user and carer involvement in formal assessment of students' practice, let alone their written work; Higher Education Institutions are likely to be reluctant to allow this (Manthorpe, 2000). Ager et al (2005) found in their 2004 audit that most of the user and carer feedback currently sought in Scottish social work programmes is indirect and not formally required. Although 75%

of the practice teachers asked said that they 'always' sought such feedback – through informal conversations, direct observation or a questionnaire – the views sought were unlikely to be representative. The authors argue that there are significant possibilities for the creative development of the role of users and carers in assessing students, including, potentially, the assessment of project work and group presentations. However, we must be aware that this presents challenges too. It requires time and resources, attention to confidentiality and representation, avoidance of tokenism, and the ability to disaggregate service issues from student practice.

The Review did identify some innovative initiatives involving users and carers in student assessment. One such initiative involves the assessments of 'user conversations', which are incorporated into the formal evaluation of students' 'safety to practice', on the new degree programme at the University of Plymouth (Elliott et al, 2005). Among the more notable initiatives in the US was the impressively early project reported by Wikler (1979), in which parents of children with learning disabilities both observed and were interviewed by social work students, rated them on the basis of these encounters, and compared their own rating priorities with those of the educators.

Modelling partnership in the student–educator relationship

An interesting strand of practice and thinking about the 'what' and the 'how' of partnership in social work education addresses the principle expressed by Preston-Shoot, that students should be recognised:

> … not as passive recipients but active determinants who share responsibility for defining clear goals and participating actively.
> *(Preston-Shoot, 1989, p 10)*

The point is taken up by other authors, arguing that if social work education about partnership work is to have meaning and integrity, it must accord with the reality of students' lived experience. Henderson (1994), for example, albeit without empirical substantiation, draws a discomforting parallel between the 'symmetrical experiences of oppression' of students and users. Huff and Johnson (1998) propose that the empowerment of students provides a model for their subsequent empowerment of users in practice.

Two reports of specific initiatives to model a partnership-based approach in the educator–student relationships are both to be found in the US. Huff and Johnson base their own conclusions on experience with second semester qualifying graduate social work students at a large south eastern university. Students worked in partnership with teachers and with each other, using learning contracts to define the scope and goals of their work, and, to an extent, determining the nature and weight of their assessment. Meanwhile Bordelon (2003) describes how the participatory learning approach adopted in a community-based project engaged him as educator/facilitator with his students in a shared and, according to his account, mutually beneficial learning experience.

2.2.6 When does education about partnership happen?

Timing of partnership work with users and carers

There is little reported debate about when students should learn about and experience partnership work with users and carers. The literature describes such initiatives at many stages of student training (Jivanjee and Friesen, 1997; Hendricks and Rudich, 2000; Pierpont et al, 2001; Bordelon, 2003). Where this work is embedded throughout programmes or courses, the principle is that partnership with users and carers should be integral to all aspects of student learning, throughout (Curran, 1997; Ager et al, 2005; Elliott et al, 2005).

Timing of interprofessional partnership work

The timing of interprofessional partnership learning is more contested, with the issue linked to concerns about the establishment and consolidation of professional identity and confidence. Glen (2001) outlines the arguments for early interprofessional learning, and those against. The findings of Pollard et al (2006: forthcoming) seem to suggest that interprofessional learning is best introduced before boundaries and stereotypes have become entrenched. Miller et al (2001), by contrast, argue that students should learn about and develop confidence in their own roles before learning about, or with, others.

2.2.7 Who benefits from education about partnership?

Status of evidence

As discussed, a majority of the studies included in the Research Review were not sufficiently empirical, or reported in sufficient detail, to be subjected to in-depth quality assessment, and their findings must therefore be treated with caution. This caveat applies all the more strongly in the case of studies that make claims about the outcomes of education about partnership. Their findings, and the conclusions drawn, may be taken only as suggestive, at best indicative, of what might be good or beneficial practice.

Benefits for students

Many papers argue the benefits of partnership education on grounds of attributed developments in students' fitness to practice, that is, their knowledge, attitudes, values and intentions, rather than the tangible demonstration of these in practice. Whether with users and carers or with other professionals, it is argued that partnership work encourages students to develop their capacities for self-reflection, and for critical reflection on practice (Curran, 1997; Pierpont et al, 2001; Trevillion and Bedford, 2003; Elliott et al, 2005). Several papers claim that students express increased appreciation of users and carers as individuals, improved understanding of their experiences and strengths, and reduced stereotyping and stigmatisation (Curran, 1997; Brandon and Knapp, 1999; Connolly and Novak, 2000; Pierpont et al, 2001). Where interprofessional education is concerned, many authors similarly contend that students develop increased knowledge and understanding of their own and others' roles, identities and perspectives, knowledges and cultures, more positive attitudes towards other professionals, and greater recognition of the potential for complementarity as well as conflict (Sklar and Torczyner, 1991; Alsop and Vigars, 1996; Barr and Waterton, 1996a, 1996b; Etchells et al, 1999; Miller et al, 2001, Maidenburg and Golick, 2001; Grossman and McCormick, 2003). It is in the context of these discussions that several of the data extracted papers, exploring the assessment of, or changes in, student attitudes and understandings of other professions, are to be located (Carpenter and Hewstone, 1996; Hyer et al, 2000; Shor and Sykes, 2002; Johnson, 2003; Colarossi and Forgey, 2006: forthcoming; Pollard et al, 2006: forthcoming). As analysis of these in section 2.3 will show, their findings in fact give a rather more mixed picture of the potential for attitude change.

Where reports do claim that the benefits of partnership learning are demonstrated in practice, this is largely in terms of practice skills. In the interprofessional partnership context, students are said to demonstrate improved collaborative, communication, conflict resolution and networking skills (Alsop and Vigars, 1996; Burns et al, 2000; Miller et al, 2001; Damon-Rodriguez and Corley, 2002; Grossman and McCormick, 2003). With users and carers, they improve their skills in listening, showing empathy and respect, acknowledging emotions and strengths, and behaving with openness and clarity (Hendricks and Rudich, 2000; Pierpont et al, 2001; Bordelon, 2003; Scheyett and Diehl, 2004; Scheyett and Kim, 2004). Only in the case of Scheyett and Kim (2004) has it been possible to subject these findings to more rigorous scrutiny (see section 2.3).

There is also some debate, as yet without conclusive evidence, about the benefits or costs of interprofessional education to students' current or future professional identity. As Barr tells us, for some, the thrust towards interprofessional learning is seen as 'a thinly disguised threat to professional identity' (Barr, 1994, p 10, cited in Atkins and Walsh, 1997). Barr and Waterton (1996a, 1996b) argue that it is only by developing and valuing role difference that effective interprofessional learning can be achieved. However, Torkington et al (2003) maintain that interprofessional learning leads not to the loss of professional identity, but to its adaptation. Trevillion and Bedford (2003), for their part, argue that one of the strong objectives and benefits of interprofessional education is that students become flexible, holistic practitioners, reflective on internal as well as external process, and imbued with a new sense of interprofessional self.

Benefits for users and carers

According to Scheyett and Diehl:

> Consumer-partnered social work education is clearly grounded in social work values and principles, but there is a need to demonstrate

that it makes a difference ... that it results in social workers who are more responsive to, and effective with, consumers of ... services than social workers provided a more traditional experience.
(Scheyett and Diehl, 2004, p 448)

While many express this hope, rarely do authors claim to establish links between service outcomes for consumers, and student learning about partnership work. Exceptions are cases such as Bordelon (2003), who considered that his students and community group partners achieved not only trusting relationships, but effective service plans far exceeding expectations. Few studies, however, are sufficiently outcome-focused let alone sufficiently rigorous to enable us to judge whether indeed partnership education 'makes a difference'.

Several papers do, however, claim to describe the positive impact on users and carers of the process of their involvement in partnership education. As service consumers, they report feeling empowered through the process of participation in social work education; they appreciate being listened to, feeling valued and recognised as individuals rather than victims (Curran, 1997; Connolly and Novak, 2000; Scheyett and Diehl, 2004; Scheyett and Kim, 2004). In one UK case, young service users have also received vocational course accreditation for their contributions (Boylan et al, 2000). In their capacity as trainers or consultants, users and carers warn of the pitfalls of tokenism, and 'consultationitis', whereby they are invited to participate too late, too minimally to make an impact, or else not for long enough to see results. Where, however, these hazards are avoided, reports suggest that users and carers express genuine enthusiasm for contributing to social work education and making a difference to the practice of the future (Boylan et al, 2000; Citizens as Trainers Group et al, 2004; Ager et al, 2005; Elliott et al, 2005).

2.3 In-depth review of studies of effectiveness

Appendix 3 summarises the 13 studies that were subject to in-depth analysis through data extraction. The aims, intervention, study design, main findings and conclusions of each study are summarised in this appendix.

2.3.1 Characteristics of the studies

Five of the 13 studies were undertaken in England and Wales, three of them in the Bristol area, one in South East England and one across England and Wales. Seven of the other eight studies were undertaken in the US, with one (Kane, 1976) also covering Canada; the eighth took place in Israel.

Table 2 shows that nearly half the studies are descriptive and two thirds involve some kind of evaluation. The studies are mainly qualitative; only two studies (Fineberg et al, 2004; Colarossi and Forgey, 2006: forthcoming) involve control groups, neither randomly allocated. Two studies include collection of follow-up data, in one case three months after the intervention (Fineberg et al, 2004), in the other, one year after qualifying (Whittington and Bell, 2001).

The 13 data extracted studies fall into two main categories: interprofessional education with a partnership focus (eight – Kane, 1976; Carpenter and Hewstone, 1996; Hyer et al, 2000; Whittington and

Table 2
Types of study included

Type of study	Number[a]
Description	6
Exploration of relationships	1
Evaluation: naturally occurring	5
Evaluation: researcher-manipulated	3

Note: [a]Two studies were rated in two categories, one as a description and an exploration of relationships, the other as a description and as a researcher-manipulated evaluation.

Bell, 2001; Johnson, 2003; Fineberg et al, 2004; Colarossi and Forgey, 2006: forthcoming; Pollard et al, 2006: forthcoming) and partnership with users in the provision of social work education with a partnership focus (five – Wikler, 1979; Jackson and Morris, 1994; Julia and Kondrat, 2000; Shor and Sykes, 2002; Scheyett and Kim, 2004). One study in each category is predominantly methodological in focus, Hyer et al (2000), addressing the validation of an instrument to measure student attitude changes related to interdisciplinary training, and Julia and Kondrat (2000) surveying social work programmes in the US to see the extent to which they address participatory and collaborative approaches to research. However, both these studies also include a substantive element, Hyer et al providing evaluation outcomes of the Geriatric Interdisciplinary Team Training (GITT), and Julia and Kondrat providing an analysis of course syllabi from 62% of MSW courses in the US.

Sample sizes are generally fairly substantial, ranging from 10 (Scheyett and Kim, 2004) to 852 (Pollard et al, 2006: forthcoming). However, the number of social workers involved in the three interdisciplinary samples is disproportionately small – in Hyer et al (2000), social workers constitute 11% of the sample, compared to 44% of medical students and 19% in nursing. In Pollard et al (2006: forthcoming) social workers make up less than 4% of the total sample and in Johnson (2003) there are only three social workers from a sample of 65. The other studies are either exclusively social workers or in three cases (Carpenter and Hewstone, 1996; Fineberg et al, 2004; Colarossi and Forgey, 2006: forthcoming), the balance of social workers with one other professional group has been deliberately constructed through sample selection. Two studies focus on programmes rather than individuals, with seven social work programmes in England and Wales included in the Jackson and Morris (1994) survey on working in partnership with families, and 75 Masters programmes in the US surveyed by Julia and Kondrat (2000).

The trustworthiness, appropriateness, relevance and overall weight of evidence (WOE) for each study was judged by the authors, as shown in Table 3, using the EPPI-Centre categories.

Table 3
Judgements on trustworthiness, appropriateness, relevance and overall WOE[1] in in-depth review

Study	A: Trust-worthy	B: Approp-riate	C: Relevance	D: Overall weight
Carpenter and Hewstone (1996)	Medium	Medium	Medium	Medium
Colarossi and Forgey (2006: forthcoming)	Medium	Medium	Medium	Medium
Fineberg et al (2004)	Medium	High	High	High
Hyer et al (2000)	High	Low	Low	Low
Jackson and Morris (1994)	Low	Low	Medium	Low
Johnson (2003)	Medium	Medium	Low	Medium
Julia and Kondrat (2000)	High	Medium	Medium	Medium
Kane (1976)	Medium	Medium	Low	Medium
Pollard et al (2006: forthcoming)	High	Medium	Low	Medium
Scheyett and Kim (2004)	Medium	Medium	High	Medium
Shor and Sykes (2002)	Medium	Medium	Medium	Medium
Whittington and Bell (2001)	Medium	Medium	High	Medium
Wikler (1979)	Low	Medium	Medium	Medium

[1] Weight of Evidence

Key to Table 3: Definitions of judgements adapted from the EPPI-Centre categories

WOE A: Taking account of all quality assessment issues, can the study findings be trusted in answering the study question(s)?

WOE B: Appropriateness of research design and analysis for addressing the question, or subquestions, of this specific systematic review.

WOE C: Relevance of particular focus of the study (including conceptual focus, context, sample and measures) for addressing the question or subquestions of this specific systematic review.

WOE D: Taking into account trustworthiness, appropriateness of design and relevance of focus, what is the overall weight of evidence this study provides to answer the question of this specific systematic review?

It should be noted that the ratings of appropriateness and relevance refer specifically to this review question and cannot be taken as a judgement of the quality of the study per se.

In the reporting of findings that follows, the overall WOE is referred to when either the one study providing high WOE or the two studies providing low WOE are discussed. All other studies provided medium WOE, which in the interests of fluency of the text is not mentioned each time the studies are discussed.

2.3.2 What do we mean by partnership in social work education?

All 13 studies make some reference to the contested nature of the concept of partnership, although mostly not using the term 'partnership' itself, a few only in the background to the study (for example, Shor and Sykes, 2002; Scheyett and Diehl, 2004, a background paper to the Scheyett and Kim, 2004 study) and others explicitly exploring concepts of partnership in the research itself (for example, Jackson and Morris, 1994). Other terms used include 'shared learning' (Carpenter and Hewstone, 1976; Whittington and Bell, 2001), 'professional identity' (Carpenter and Hewstone, 1976; Johnson, 2003), 'shared leadership' (Hyer et al,

2000, providing low WOE), 'collaboration', 'teamwork' (Kane, 1976) and 'participation' (Scheyett and Diehl, 2004; Scheyett and Kim, 2004). Scheyett and Diehl (2004, p 436) suggest that:

> In social work practice, 'partnership' is conceptualized as a collaborative process whereby the social worker and client work as equals, each with areas of strength and expertise, each with the ability to exercise autonomy and choice.

No definitive position about the interchangeability of the various terms used emerges from the evidence. Scheyett and Diehl (2004) seem to be distinguishing between service users' and carers' *participation* in the process of social work education and full *partnership* in which service users' expertise around their experiences, needs and preferences are acknowledged, sought out and actively incorporated into the curriculum. They argue that by increasing participation and equalising the power base, 'true partnership' is more likely to be established. However, elsewhere in this Review it is acknowledged that service users and carers are often involuntary 'partners', for example, because of statutory requirements, suggesting that Scheyett and Diehl's definition is more aspirational than descriptive of reality. This focus on power is reflected in the Tunnard definition given in the introduction and from the studies reviewed. Jackson and Morris (1994) note that tutors referred to the power differentials between social workers and the families with whom they work, arguing that the term 'partnership' could never be appropriate in that situation. Contrastingly, Scheyett and Kim's (2004) study demonstrated that through the use of facilitated 'structured dialogue', students reported intended changes in practice around developing partnership.

Only one study in the 13, providing low WOE, explored the definition of partnership empirically (Jackson and Morris, 1994), and asked social work students, tutors and practice teachers about their definition, concepts and coverage of partnership in seven qualifying programmes in England and Wales. Most respondents (students, tutors and practice teachers) had difficulties articulating a definition of partnership, with many of the students not answering this question. The replies received characterised partnership in terms of sharing power, joint decision making and recognition of respective roles and responsibilities. The conclusions argue strongly for greater transparency of the concept of partnership, acknowledging that it has different meanings in different contexts, without which teaching of partnership will be ineffective and difficult for students, practice teachers and tutors to evaluate.

2.3.3 Why is partnership work important in social work education?

The studies justify the focus on partnership with reference to legislative and more general policy requirements, changes in training requirements, a more holistic approach to service users' needs and the increasing empowerment agenda. For example, on interprofessional education with a partnership focus, Colarossi and Forgey (2006: forthcoming), in the context of domestic violence in the US, refer to 'the need for coordination of services requiring collaboration among the various professionals operating them' (draft, p 3). Johnson (2003) refers to Department of Health policy in England, in noting the intention for interprofessional education to provide a key role in joint training in core skills such as communication. Changing demographics, such as the growing numbers of elderly service users, demand that professionals work together to meet complex medical and social needs (Hyer et al, 2000, providing low WOE). These demands are not new; the most dated paper included in the data extraction by Rosalie Kane (1976) documents this debate in Master's degree level social work in the US in the 1970s.

In relation to partnership with service users and carers, the rationale is also to be found in legislative and policy frameworks, as noted in section 2.2. Scheyett and Diehl (2004) report that in the US, the Council of Social Work Education (CSWE) policy statement emphasises the worth and dignity of service users as a basis for building professional relationships. The role is 'not to do *for*, but rather *with* clients' (Scheyett and Diehl, 2004, p 436). In justification of their studies of improving attitudes towards consumers, Scheyett and Kim (2004) and Shor and Sykes (2002) suggest that positive attitudes of social workers towards service users are essential for effective intervention. Jackson and Morris (1994, providing low WOE) raise similar points.

2.3.4 Who does partnership in social work education involve?

Eight of the 13 studies focus on aspects of interprofessional education. Of these, one is a wide-scale survey of interprofessional education in social work programmes (Kane, 1976), but its generalisability to the current Review is limited by having been undertaken in 1974 and in the US. One (Whittington and Bell, 2001) focuses just on social workers' attitudes towards other disciplines, whereas five others (Carpenter and Hewstone, 1996; Hyer et al, 2000; Johnson, 2003; Fineberg et al, 2004, providing high WOE; Pollard et al, 2006: forthcoming) are predominantly about social workers' attitudes towards, and experience of, healthcare staff. Colarossi and Forgey (2006: forthcoming) focus on social work and law students.

Of the seven studies which focus on changes in knowledge and attitudes following specific interdisciplinary training or in one case (Whittington and Bell, 2001), following experiences at work after qualifying, all have some positive findings to report, although several also note some attitudes becoming more negative. Whittington and Bell followed social workers one year after qualifying and found that they worked with a wide range of organisations and other professionals and experienced serious gaps in how well equipped they felt themselves to do so. They reported feeling well-understood by other social workers and by some other professionals such as nurses and health visitors. However, those they felt least well understood by were doctors, police and solicitors, the same groups with whom they were least likely to experience shared learning and yet with whom they had a great deal of professional contact.

Of three studies (Carpenter and Hewstone, 1996; Fineberg et al, 2004; Colarossi and Forgey, 2006: forthcoming), one (Fineberg et al, 2004, providing high WOE) utilised variations on pre/post test designs to measure knowledge, understanding and attitudes before and after interdisciplinary training inputs. Johnson (2003) collected data following an input. Pollard et al (2006: forthcoming) followed a major cohort of students from a range of disciplines through the same input, taking measures at regular intervals. These five studies provide a very mixed picture of the effects of interprofessional education that focuses on partnership. The three measuring changes are able to demonstrate improved knowledge and attitudes, although in the Colarossi and Forgey study (2006: forthcoming) improved attitudes were to issues relating to domestic violence and attitudes towards interdisciplinary work made no improvement. Fineberg et al (2004, providing high WOE), note an increase in perceived understanding of professional roles that was maintained at the three-month follow-up and was significantly greater than in the control group. However, the authors note that as in all the other studies, measurements were limited to perceived knowledge and professional roles, not actual practice. Carpenter and Hewstone (1996) conclude that attitudes can be changed through shared learning, but this cannot remove all the barriers, some of which they acknowledge are structural. In just under one fifth of their sample, the programme did not demonstrate positive effects and attitudes worsened.

Johnson (2003) and Pollard et al (2006: forthcoming) also report very mixed outcomes, although both these studies have relatively small numbers of social workers involved. Lack of clarity about the purpose of interprofessional education was a particular complaint in the Johnson sample; the author also notes the tension between uniprofessional and interprofessional education, claiming that 'too much work, too little time and unclear priorities' (2003, p 318) were the problem. Similarly, many of those in the Pollard et al sample expressed mixed views, with more positive views of interprofessional learning and much more negative ones expressed about interprofessional practice. The authors suggest that recent high-profile failures in the services may have contributed to this and acknowledge that without a comparison or control group it is difficult to attribute these views to the programme itself.

Of the five studies reviewed that focus on partnership with service users and carers, one is about partnership with parents of children with learning disabilities (Wikler, 1979), one is generic as it focuses on participatory approaches in courses (Julia and Kondrat, 2000), two focus on users of mental health services (Shor and Sykes, 2002; Scheyett and Kim, 2004) and the other on families (Jackson and Morris,1994, providing low WOE).

The process of negotiation between practice teacher, tutor and student, in setting up placements, itself provides a basis for partnership learning that Jackson and Morris (1994) suggest could be better recognised and developed as such. They report that the use of consumer feedback for assessment purposes in practice placements is particularly helpful. Wikler (1979) similarly notes the usefulness of the consumer, in this case parents' feedback to students on their interview skills, and Scheyett and Kim (2004) and Shor and Sykes (2002) report on informal feedback from consumers of mental health services on a facilitated dialogue with social work students.

2.3.5 What does partnership in social work education include, and how is it included?

What is included?

Studies in this Review with a specific focus include Colarossi and Forgey (2006: forthcoming), who focus on domestic violence, Fineberg et al (2004, providing high WOE), which looks at training in palliative care, Jackson and Morris (1994, providing low WOE), focusing on families and child protection, Scheyett and Kim (2004) and Shor and Sykes (2002), who report on consumers of mental health services, Wikler (1979) whose focus is parents of those with learning disabilities, and Hyer et al (2000, providing low WOE), whose focus is interdisciplinary training for geriatric services. Jackson and Morris (1994), in a relevant but relatively methodologically limited study, note that all seven social work programmes surveyed explore partnership in relation to child protection but none in relation to residential care; they note, too, that residential care was little covered at all (not just in relation to partnership), and argue that this reflects its status as a 'Cinderella' area of social work. Preparation of family members to participate in case conferences also received less attention than was deemed necessary by students. Almost all respondents in their study reported that concepts of partnership were integrated throughout the teaching programme. Some suggested that it was evident in most of the programmes, whereas one stated: 'It must have been integrated because we didn't notice it' (Jackson and Morris, 1994, p 5).

Jackson and Morris (1994) also report that coverage of the implications of 'race', class, religion, culture and language was seen as important in developing partnership practice, although students felt that programmes could only cover certain aspects in the time (Jackson and Morris, 1994). 'Race' and language were covered in all programmes they reviewed, but disability, sexuality, class, religion and culture had limited coverage. The authors argue that if there is little explicit teaching in this area, an understanding of how oppression can create barriers to partnership working will not be grasped.

Several of the studies attempt to identify the skills needed in partnership work. For example, Whittington and Bell (2001) identify 13 skills that included communication, negotiating conflict, managing multidisciplinary meetings and using networks. However, for all the skills identified, the social workers rated their prior training as less effective in securing them than the rating of importance that they allocated to each skill. They felt ill-equipped to handle conflict, to adapt to change in other organisations or to run multidisciplinary meetings. Students, tutors and practice teachers in Jackson and Morris's study (providing low WOE), suggested that counselling, empathy, respect, advocacy and empowerment were important skills for interprofessional work. They also suggested that they need skills in approaches to involving families, particularly in developing and using written agreements about the services they are to receive. These researchers asked respondents to identify skills needed to overcome barriers to partnership, but most respondents found it difficult to identify any; this may reflect Carpenter and Hewstone's (1996) conclusion that some of the barriers are structural rather than reflecting attitudes.

How is partnership addressed?

The 13 studies reviewed in depth address coverage of partnership in two ways. Some studies focus on what messages about partnership should be included and how far these are integrated through the curriculum or separately addressed in a block identified as 'partnership'. Johnson (2003) contrasts technical skills in social work with skills required for interdisciplinary work such as collaboration, empathy and empowerment. Jackson and Morris (1994, providing low WOE) argue that reconsideration should be given to addressing partnership more explicitly rather than losing it or diluting it through integration.

Other studies focus on interprofessional partnership, comparing the benefits of different professionals learning alongside one another with those of developing a strong professional identity through learning with others from the same profession. Glen (2001), in a conceptual paper not included in the in-depth analysis, argues cogently that lack of clarity about the priorities of interprofessional education will lead to resentment and a perception that learning opportunities are being diluted, as indeed reported in Johnson (2003) and Pollard et al (2006: forthcoming). Kane (1976) concludes that the objective of interprofessional education is to enable students to establish and keep their own identities and to develop collaborative ones alongside them: 'combined understandings but separate talents' (p 237). By far the strongest message from several of these studies is the difficulty of *fitting it all in*.

In an interesting paper that describes a monitoring exercise rather than a study (and hence has not been reviewed in depth), Gronski and Pigg (2000) note that limited attention was paid to authentic collaborative skill development in departments providing professional training across one university. Programmes tended to be limited to the acquisition of technical competence in a single discipline with no coordination across departments of field experience activities within the same localities. The researchers argue that the universities should be strengthening the development of civic society by helping to solve complex problems through integrating collaborative skills into technical professional education.

Supporting the development of partnership work

The conclusions of the studies reviewed identify a number of processes that seem to support effective education for partnership work, either interprofessional or with service users and carers. In several studies focusing on partnership in interprofessional education, the value of tutors from different disciplines modelling partnership behaviour is emphasised (for example, Fineberg et al, 2004, providing high WOE; Colarossi and Forgey, 2006: forthcoming). Clarity of purpose in provision for interprofessional training (Jackson and Morris, 1994, providing low WOE; Johnson, 2003) also emerges as a key factor in supporting or inhibiting partnership in interprofessional education.

Whittington and Bell (2001) note that practice-based learning and post-qualification work experience were perceived as contributing most to interprofessional competences, a finding endorsed by Jackson and Morris (1994) who conclude that the programmes which linked the teaching of partnership with practice experience were more effective. Whittington and Bell further report that the Certificate in Social Service (CSS) trained social workers rated their academic training more highly than those trained in the Certificate of Qualification in Social Work

(CQSW). As CSS students tended to be older, the authors suggest that maturity, experience and organisational acclimatisation may all have contributed to these differences.

Wikler (1979), Scheyett and Kim (2004) and Shor and Sykes (2002) demonstrated supporting and developing partnership with service users and carers. These studies provide support for the involvement of service users and carers in training social workers. Although none include follow-up measures of subsequent practice, Scheyett and Kim report positively on students' intentions to change their practice. Wikler concludes that the most important skill enhanced by this process was 'really listening' (p 149). All three studies stress the value of social work students seeing service users and carers outside of a crisis situation and thereby appreciating their strengths and skills. Shor and Sykes note that two thirds of the social work students in their study felt that the 'structured dialogue' with people with mental illness 'opened their eyes to the person behind the illness' (p 67). Scheyett and Kim refer to 'consumer recovery' – the fact that mental illness can be a temporary not permanent characterising state – as a concept that students need to understand in order to emphasise the process of moving on and actively contending with the disorder or disability. However, in the Scheyett and Kim study, the students reported some confusion about how to create healthy appropriate boundaries in their professional work. Given that the 'structured dialogue' intervention that was adopted in this study was short (similarly so in the Shor and Sykes study), only of one day's duration, it seems likely that lack of experience contributed to this difficulty.

There is little evidence that research addressing partnership was assimilated into the learning of students about partnership; Jackson and Morris (1994, low WOE) found that programmes were more likely to refer to guidance or regulations than to research. Students favoured active learning through case studies and workshops, although evidence from reviews of professional development in other fields (for example, Robinson and Sebba, 2004) suggests this is true of teaching in general, not just that focused on partnership. Julia and Kondrat (2000) concluded that 'graduate social work research syllabi and textbooks have little coverage of either specific methods of participatory research or concepts related to empowerment in the research process' (p 113). This, they argue, is at odds with the emphasis and professional expectation of collaboration in work with service users.

None of the seven social work education programmes reviewed by Jackson and Morris reported a formal monitoring system for the teaching of partnership. Likewise there was very little evidence from any of the studies reviewed of monitoring or evaluation on a regular basis, by service or training providers, of partnership skills taught. Again, this finding is characteristic of findings from professional development research in general but has implications for longer-term provision. Jackson and Morris link this issue firmly back to the definitional one, by questioning how, without clarity of definition, students, service users and carers or providers will be able to judge effectiveness. Hyer et al (2000), in a robust but less directly relevant study, demonstrated the potential use of attitudinal scales in measuring changes following interprofessional training in geriatric care in their validation of the 'Attitudes Towards Health Care Teams Scale' (ATHCTS). This study includes a large sample of social workers (98), and demonstrated changes in attitudes in three areas that were defined as the value of the team, team efficiency and shared leadership.

2.3.6 When does education about partnership work happen?

Schon (1987) suggests that experiential learning for collaborative skill development should become central to the core of university professional training to prepare professionals for the demands of a complex society. Gronski and Pigg's (2000) contention that complex problems can only be addressed through the development of better integrated collaborative skills across the university, similarly places the responsibility with Higher Education for the early integration of partnership skills. The evidence from the 13 studies reviewed in-depth does not as yet provide unequivocal support for the specific timing of introducing partnership work; however, no studies comparing timing as such were identified.

Carpenter and Hewstone (1996) suggest that social workers and doctors improved their knowledge and attitudes of each other's roles and duties through shared learning at the qualifying stages, which they propose are necessary conditions for collaboration in practice. Fineberg et al (2004, providing high WOE) similarly conclude that the experiential exercises promoting interdisciplinary working undertaken by social work and medical students offered 'a viable method for introducing early interdisciplinary exposure and socialisation', (p 10). They argue that professional socialisation in interdisciplinary work can be influenced early in the development process. Johnson (2003) similarly argues for early introduction of interprofessional education, although her data are too ambivalent to support this outright. She acknowledges that her findings support her contention that strategies will be needed to accompany this early introduction, to enhance its perceived relevance and clarity. The finding that older students hold more negative views of interprofessional interaction (Pollard et al, 2006: forthcoming) suggests support for earlier introduction, so long as it is possible to establish that coverage or experience of interprofessional work do not lead to greater negativity. The implication in Pollard et al's finding is that professional identities become more entrenched (what Pollard et al refer to as 'stereotype formation' through uniprofessional education) and less flexible over time, necessitating some 'undoing' of attitudes and ways of working prior to developing interprofessional partnership. A more constructive approach implied by these findings is to introduce interprofessional experience earlier, thus promoting interprofessional partnership from the outset and preventing the necessity to challenge entrenched views later.

Practice Survey

3.1 Aims and scope of the Practice Survey

The purpose of the Practice Survey, in line with guidance from SCIE, was to review current practice and map the emerging arrangements for the learning, teaching and assessment of partnership work by providers of social work education in the three UK countries covered by SCIE: England, Wales and Northern Ireland.

3.2 Methodology

3.2.1 Sources of information

Three strategies were designed to enable a 'drilling down' approach with providers of the new degrees and their stakeholders, moving from the construction of an initial 'map' or base line of partnership work, to in-depth telephone interviews with providers where there was an indication of good practice, through to a detailed analysis of examples of learning, teaching and assessment of partnership work with programmes and stakeholders at programme level.

3.2.2 Survey of programme and module handbooks

The intention of the initial survey of programme and module handbooks was to 'map' the territory of the learning, teaching and assessment of 'partnership work'. In adopting this strategy it was hoped to avoid exacerbating the anticipated research fatigue of the community. The 'map' would address the broad levels of partnership but beyond this would not attempt a qualitative analysis.

A letter about the Practice Survey (see Appendix 4) was mailed to 78 social work 'programme directors' in England, Wales and Northern Ireland, representing the total number of providers of the new degree at BA or MA/postgraduate levels at the time of the study. The letter was sent to a named member of staff who appeared to be responsible for the new degree in each institution – by scrutinising websites and following up with clarifying telephone calls, efforts were made to ensure appropriate people were identified, although this was not always successful.

The letter informed programme directors of the research and requested copies of relevant programme documentation and 'operational' literature used by educators and stakeholders, including, for example, programme and module handbooks. Of these, 33 were returned in time for inclusion in this Review, representing a return rate of 41%. Documentation provided ranged from a complete set of programme and module handbooks to one module handbook. The return rate was lower than hoped for and was only achieved as a result of follow-up activity by the research officer. Conversations had during follow-up telephone calls with programme directors indicated both research fatigue as well as general fatigue as a result of the major changes underway in social work education (see section 3.3.2).

3.2.3 Telephone survey

The original intention was to seek telephone interviews with 15 of the providers who submitted documentation. The main criteria for inclusion were those where initial analysis of the documentation indicated 'good practice' in the learning, teaching and assessment of partnership work. In addition, criteria included:

- geographic spread, including representation from the three UK countries involved and from different regions of the UK;
- a sample of both undergraduate and postgraduate programmes in England (at this time there were no postgraduate qualifying social work programmes in Wales or Northern Ireland).

The researchers requested follow-up telephone interviews with a sample of 16 respondents. Telephone interviews using a semi-structured questionnaire (see Appendix 6) were conducted with the 14 respondents who agreed, a response rate of 87%. These included one programme in Northern Ireland, one in Wales, 12 from different regions of England, 11 undergraduate and five postgraduate and two that combine undergraduate and postgraduate. On occasions, telephone interviews resulted in respondents sending further programme documentation, usually at module level.

3.2.4 Focus groups

Based on an analysis of the telephone interviews, the intention was to undertake five focus groups on sites of 'good practice' to explore teaching learning and assessment of partnership work (see section 3.3.4 for a discussion of 'good practice'). The original plan was to establish three separate focus groups on each site: students; users and carers; academic staff and practice assessors/teachers. Furthermore, the plan was to include users and carers as well as academic researchers and practitioner researchers in the research teams to enable focus group interviews to be led by relevant team members and so address power relations and enable participants to share their views as freely as possible. Following a meeting of the stakeholder group (see section 1.5), University of Sussex postgraduates and University of Sussex/University of Brighton undergraduates joined the research team. The research team also planned to explore and model its own partner processes.

Six possible sites were approached for focus groups but the reality of complexities in planning and holding a focus group was a disincentive to participation. One site, although very interested in participating, could not make it happen in the time available in a context where almost all staff had changed during the previous year, students were at the university for one day per week only and the university had just undergone major restructuring. The second site, also interested, eventually declined on the basis of what they perceived as lack of sufficiently clear project information for service users and carers. (As a result of this, the relevant project information was overhauled.) In the event, four focus groups were undertaken due to what might be considered as some of the realities of partnership work. The focus groups included four groups of students (total 30), three focus groups with service users and carers (total 25), and four meetings with academic staff and practice educators (total 10).

In consultation with SCIE, the research team decided to 'streamline' the focus groups and adapt the ideal model to a more pragmatic approach and not require the three sets of stakeholders to be available for each visit, but rather target specific stakeholders depending on the focus of the visit. Focus groups were therefore conducted using topics particularly relevant to the specific site and target group.

Site 1

An academic researcher interviewed six academic and practice learning staff. A service user and an academic researcher interviewed two practice managers. A practitioner researcher and a service user interviewed 15 MA students. A service user and a practitioner researcher interviewed four service users.

Site 2

An academic researcher interviewed two academic programme convenors (Social Work and Nursing) for a Level Two BA Partnership module. A Level Two BA student member of the research team led the interview with five BA Level Two students, supported by an academic researcher.

Site 3

An academic researcher interviewed the member of academic staff responsible for managing the programme, attended a meeting of the Service User and Carer Consultative Group and also attended a meeting of students with the programme director. The Consultative Group consisted of 15 service users and carers, as well as members of the academic staff, some of whom were responsible for practice learning. The student group consisted of seven students, three second years and four first years.

Site 4

A practitioner researcher interviewed the programme director (and module convenor). A student member of the research team interviewed a student group of three. A practitioner/researcher and a carer from the research team interviewed a group of six users and carers.

3.2.5 Confidentiality, bias and ethics

Respondents to the programme survey, the telephone interviews and the focus groups were identified by name in the returns but all personally identifying information has been removed in analysing and reporting on the data for this review. All contributors of good practice examples are named with their knowledge and written consent.

The research officer, a practitioner new to research, was not familiar with the national social work education field prior to the survey and was not known to the respondents. The two other Practice Survey researchers were experienced social work educators and, as a result, attention was paid to possible sources of bias in the selection of respondents for telephone interviews and focus groups, the choice of questions asked, the data analysis and reporting of findings. This meant that where a researcher was well known to the respondents, the intention was for another member of the research team to undertake the telephone interview and/or the focus group. Similarly, the intention was that researchers unfamiliar with the site undertook data analysis in relation to specific sites. In the large majority of cases this was implemented; however, towards the end of the data collection period when time was short and the team was working intensively to increase the data available, a decision was made to proactively use individual networks and obtain data, which meant that three telephone interviews were undertaken by a researcher known to the programme director.

Every effort was made to ensure that service users and carers and students were adequately informed about the research prior to interviews and that appropriate information was available from project letters (see Appendix 4) and/or from on-site programme directors, who proved enormously helpful to the project team. The issues of consent and informed consent were addressed in the original invitation letter to service users and carers and to students as well as in a simple consent form that was distributed on the day to those taking part (see Appendix 5). All participants signed the consent forms.

Payments were made to most participating service users and carers and book tokens (£15.00) were distributed to participating students.

3.2.6 Data analysis

Data from the programme and module handbooks and the interviews were analysed using thematic manual analysis (see section 2.1.6). Originally it had been the intention to use SPSS, but in the event the data were very mixed and difficult to quantify and compare. Almost all focus groups were tape-recorded and the tapes transcribed prior to analysis of the data. Key concerns, themes and debates were identified from repeated reading of the transcript material by the academic researchers and the practitioner researcher, with subsequent organisation of the data into a thematic framework.

3.3 Four factors that shaped the course of the Practice Survey

3.3.1 Shifting boundaries of the study

The focus of the study agreed with SCIE was the 'learning, teaching and assessment of partnership work'. SCIE wished to exclude interprofessional education as a form of partnership as this was to be the topic of a future commission. However, it was agreed that if the interprofessional programme focused on the learning, teaching and assessment of *partnership* work this would be included. It was also agreed with SCIE that 'partnership' as reflected in the programme structure would not be included. As will become clear in the following discussion, it proved very difficult to maintain these boundaries. The emphasis on partnership as a value, on its embedded nature and on the importance of 'modelling' partnership all contribute to it being viewed holistically across an entire programme rather than in discrete sections.

3.3.2 Research fatigue in the field

There were clear indications that the field of social work education was becoming saturated by requests for engagement in research and that programme leaders, already overstretched by managing the social work education change process, found it difficult to prioritise participating in yet one more survey.

This e-mail from a programme director whose lack of response to a request for a focus group was being followed up is indicative of that of other programme directors who were very supportive of the research but felt unable to participate due to pressure of work:

> In the last few weeks, students have been involved in focus groups to evaluate practice learning and the programme thus far, focus groups about the supply and demand of social care education and focus groups for the five-year review and I think we are very likely to hit focus group fatigue!

Paradoxically, the experience of the research team was that once participants were engaged in discussion, interviews often continued for longer than contracted for and in telephone interviews and focus groups respondents reported finding the discussion helpful.

3.3.3 Tacit knowledge

The research team was aware of the significance in professional practice of tacit knowledge, not necessarily readily accessible in a questionnaire or interview (see section 1.3). This dynamic, combined with the conceptual confusion in the field and the continuing need to clarify the focus of 'partnership work', meant that it was essential to ask different participants in social work education for their views and to provide examples, in an attempt to triangulate the data. Opportunities for such exploration were limited given time constraints and the limits of the study.

3.3.4 'Good practice'

'Good practice' is an elusive concept. Preliminary analyses of programme handbook data revealed that they were not reliable sources of data about the learning, teaching and assessment of 'partnership'. 'Partnership' was often invisible, other than referenced in the programme structure, even when data from other sources suggested that the learning, teaching and assessment of partnership work were on offer. When it was referred to in the handbooks, the emphasis was on the 'what' rather than the 'how' or 'why'. Analysis of module handbooks indicated that partnership work was in progress, but statements typically written in the outcomes language of the QAA rarely more than hinted at anything that might be construed as 'good practice'. One programme director in a telephone interview argued for the need to develop a new language of partnership that was different from everyday understanding.

The research team agreed to introduce criteria for good practice against which potential examples could be rated. Two or more criteria would be expected to be present before a programme would be selected for a telephone interview. The telephone interview would then enquire further against the criteria, resulting in identifying sites of good practice for focus groups. Criteria 1-4 below were identified in the original research proposal. Criteria 5-7 were added following an important stakeholder group discussion of 'good practice':

1. Service user and carer involvement in programme design or delivery.
2. Teaching, learning and assessment of partnership work specifically identified.
3. Innovative features in the design or delivery of teaching, learning and assessment of partnership work.
4. Partnership work and the new degree disseminated in the public domain through refereed conference presentations or journal articles, with a particular focus on abstracts for the Joint Social Work Education Conferences of 2003, 2004 and the related Themed Editions of *Social Work Education* (2004, vol 23, no 2; 2005, vol 24, no 4).
5. Consideration of partnership with other professionals.
6. Consideration of what was the 'pay off' for service users and carers.
7. Evidence of research or evaluation of partnership practice.

3.4 Themes emerging from the Practice Survey

To summarise, data was obtained from the following sources.

33 programme handbooks
18 undergraduate only, including one undergraduate programme from Northern Ireland and one undergraduate from Wales.
10 postgraduate and undergraduate, England only.

5 postgraduate, England only.

9 module handbooks
These handbooks were very varied. They ranged from whole courses to single sessions with no discernible pattern of when they were offered during undergraduate or postgraduate programmes:
Theory, Methods and Values, which included learning and teaching about partnership work.
Skills courses, which focused on communication with users and carers and/or professional groups.
'Professional practice' courses that discussed partnership and profesional boundaries.
Multiagency and interdisciplinary working.
Partnership in a specific field of practice, for example, community care.
Partnership working and management.

15 telephone interviews
7 undergraduate only, including one each in Northern Ireland and Wales.
6 undergraduate and postgraduate, England only.
2 postgraduate, England only.

4 focus groups
1 undergraduate, England.
3 undergraduate and postgraduate, England.

The following themes emerge from the sources of data (coded as follows):
Handbook analysis (HBA)

Module handbook analysis (MHBA)

Telephone interviews (TI)

Focus group academic (FGA)

Focus group practitioners (FGP)

Focus group students (FGS)

ocus group service user/carer (FGSUC)

The data source is identified, but findings are not differentiated according to data source, consistent with the 'drilling down' strategy. Each theme is introduced with a brief explanation of the meaning of the theme. To simplify reporting and in the interests of word length, each theme includes the findings as well as discussion of what they might mean.

3.4.1 What do we mean by partnership?

The first question that inevitably had to be clarified in discussion with participants was how the research team defined partnership (see section 1.4). The research team attempted to seek the respondents' definition first and to then re-focus if the respondents' focus was on aspects of partnership beyond the survey.

It was illuminating to note where participants began. Most frequently, partnership was defined either in terms of work with other professionals or work with service users and carers, or both. Partnership was not defined as a curriculum topic in its own right.

Academic and practice staff identified partnership as:

> … an umbrella term embracing different relationships, complex and under-theorised and therefore often not recognised.
> *(TI)*

The following discussion explores the meaning of partnership in three main ways reflecting the predominant ways that respondents discussed partnership (TI, FGA): how partnership is linked to social work values and anti-oppressive practice (AOP), its contested nature and its evolution in social work education.

a) Partnership, AOP and values
i) Working anti-oppressively is fundamental to partnership work
Educators referred to partnership as being explicitly linked to AOP in three different ways: as an essential aspect of AOP; as a process that needs constant attention; and in danger of being talked about rather than delivered:

If practice is not informed by AOP we will not be able to put partnership into action.
(TI)

Involving stakeholders in teaching has to be continually worked on, like AOP in the DipSW.
(TI)

There is a danger of paying lip service to partnership. It was suggested that people responded to it tokenistically.
(FGA 1)

A group of students also discussed the links between partnership and AOP:

Partnership is about giving up power.
(FGS 3)

A group of Level One undergraduate students, yet to go on placement, informally discussing a partnership module during a coffee break discussed partnership as 'common sense'.

The risk of such views is that they are reductionist and ignore issues of power and oppression and the impact of structural barriers on partnership.

ii) Partnership is congruent with social work values
Students in three focus groups made connections between partnership and social work values. The following brief dialogue between two Level Two undergraduate students illustrates this:

It comes down to basic respect for each other.

Yes it comes down to the basic standards and humanist principles of social work really.

Partnership was also discussed by users and carers who described their collaboration with a social work programme from a values perspective:

> Everyone is equal, everyone works together.
> *(FGSUC 4)*

b) Partnership as contested

Educators suggest that partnership is a 'contested' term. It was suggested that this might be particularly relevant to relating theory to practice where cultures and priorities could be different. A focus group of educators concluded that the term is inherently problematic because practice is behind in thinking about partnership, and therefore students have to be prepared for something that is difficult or impossible to deliver (FGA 1). A programme director in another university suggested that the emphasis in practice on performance outcomes is not compatible with partnership, as partnership stresses process and relationship. Partnership is seen as antithetical to prevailing cultures, which are managerialist and emphasise performance measurement (TI). A third programme director suggested that partnership might be about creating new organisations and structures, requiring different models for different client groups and different agencies (TI).

Students in two focus groups from different universities also viewed partnership as problematic in practice:

> It works well here [university], what we are taught is best practice. I think the barriers we are going to come up against most are the practice attitudes that exist in social work.... We've been taught to work in conjunction with social workers in other agencies and for a consensus to be reached and that's not the attitude of the majority of the social workers whose teams we are working in. To fight against that is going to be one of the great problems. But I am not sure that battling against those attitudes is something that can be taught on a course. I think it's about being strong enough to say that's what I believe in and this is the way this should be done, to your colleagues. Which is a hard thing to do when they have a lot more seniority and experience but just because they've got seniority and experience doesn't mean they are doing things the right way.
> *(FGS 1)*

c) The evolution of partnership in social work education practice

In understanding the meaning of 'partnership' to programme staff the legacy of the DipSW must be taken into account, particularly in terms of relationships with agencies and with service users and carers. For example, one university, where learning about 'partnership' was specifically identified as being provided in a context of interprofessional working, had been working on these ideas for several years prior to the new degree. Here a 'hub' group of users and carers had existed before the degree and took part in its planning. At the time of the telephone interview this included 16 users and carers (TI).

A programme director referred to building on the past but also having an opportunity for a 'clean slate'. Doing things differently in the degree emerged most strongly in relation to partnership with users and carers:

> We took some conscious decisions at the start about service users and carers, we were going to do it properly, we weren't going to rush it and we wanted it to be as useful as possible in terms of the programme and we also wanted to ensure that we had the broadest definition of what partnerships are. Because, after all, we were only a year away from partnership meaning local authorities.
> *(FGA 3)*

The differentiation is commonly shared between a DipSW partnership being between universities and local authorities and partnership in the new degree emphasising users and carers. The extent of involvement of users and carers is variable.

> It's not about involving service users but service users being in control and involved with social workers. I suppose our thinking is sometimes quite a way beyond early thinking about ideas of partnership.
> *(TI)*

3.4.2 Why is partnership in social work education important?

The rationale for the learning, teaching and assessment of partnership work in social work education is almost invisible in programme handbooks. Programme philosophy is infrequently stated and typically does not refer to partnership work in spite of structures that clearly identify programme 'partners'. The three possible reasons for this are:

- 'Partnership' is understood rather than explicit, having been required for the DipSW since 1990 as part of the requirement for partnership with employers.
- Partnership is an explicit requirement of accrediting bodies and UK governments so the rationale may be assumed to be self-evident.
- Partnership is viewed as a valuable activity that does not require a rationale, in spite of lack of evidence of its effectiveness (Glasby and Lester, 2004).

Examples of the conviction about the value of learning about partnership work is expressed by these practitioners in a focus group:

The more our students work with other professions and have an understanding of the wider social context, the better they will be as social workers.

Partnership is essential because of the nature of organisations, the way practice is and will be.

Collaborative working is required by government. Integrated teams require interdisciplinary working, interdisciplinary teams need partnership.
(FGP 1)

These statements contrast with the sceptical views of partnership in practice expressed by educators in section 3.4.1.

3.4.3 Who should partnership in social work education involve?

There was a range of responses to the question about who is included in partnership relationships. The responses primarily fell into either partnership with users and carers or with other agencies and professions, or both. The initial comments of students in one focus group illustrate this point:

What came to my mind was partnership between social servicᴖ, education and health. That was what I was thinking of. (FGS 4)

I was thinking about partnership with voluntary organisations in the community. On this course we have had people from a woman's refuge talk to us, we had a chap come from a disabled organisation. I was thinking along those lines that they would have some important things to teach on the course.
(FGS 1)

As indicated in the introduction, partnership was initially conceptualised in the research proposal as occurring at four broad 'levels':

1. Social work student and service user/carer
2. Student and educator/assessor
3. Educator/assessor and stakeholder, including users/carers, employers and practitioners
4. Higher Education Institution and stakeholder.

An early finding from all three stages of the Practice Survey was that there were three further levels:

1. Social work student and student from another profession
2. Groups of social work students on courses
3. Social work academics and academics from another profession

As the study progressed, the term 'level' proved too linear and boundaried because the stakeholders do not conceptualise partnership as occurring within one course or module or as occurring with either other professions or with users and carers. Rather there is a complex set of interacting matrices or systems, which include a range of relevant relationships. Hence in the following discussion some partners have been grouped together.

Partnership between social work educator and service user/carer

Much of the data in focus groups and telephone interviews is about partnership between educators and service users and carers, suggesting that this is a dominant issue. This emphasis is only partially explained by the research team's efforts to avoid a focus on interprofessional education.

The research identified numerous examples of service users and carers being involved in different aspects of course development and delivery. Some of these were specific such as teaching sessions or involvement in selecting new students. However, there were fewer examples of comprehensive involvement, including assessment and managing and delivering complete modules as demonstrated by the following practice examples.

Practice example 1: Service user and carer involvement

University of Plymouth BSc Hons Health and Social Care Management

Multi-Disciplinary Working

This group meets regularly with university staff. It has been involved in planning the new award and continues to play a significant role in all aspects of delivery and development. It contributes to partnership learning in a number of ways:

1. The service user 'conversation': service users and carers take part in assessing whether students are Safe for Practice. The student writes an account of their view of the 'qualities of a good social worker'. They receive formative feedback 'in conversation' with a service user or carer. Students are given the opportunity to respond to this feedback, which is then evaluated by the same service user and the outcome of their view affects the marking process. A wide range of service users and carers are involved. Consideration is being given to developing this initiative by videoing or taping the conversation so students can continue building on their learning. (For more detail see Elliott et al, 2005.)
2. Service users and carers are involved in the substantial two-week induction at the beginning of the course, which includes a session explaining why service users are involved.

This emphasis on the contribution of service users defines the culture of the whole course.

3. Service users and carers are involved in the substantial two-week induction at the beginning of the course, which includes a session explaining why service users are involved. This emphasis on the contribution of service users defines the culture of the whole course.

4. Service users take part in teaching sessions. While there has been positive feedback from students, this involvement takes a lot of time, both during the session and in preparation.

5. Service users have been involved in formative assessment. The practice portfolio includes a care plan or review. One service user discusses these plans with a group of three or four students and gives feedback to each student from a service user perspective. Students are expected to note and respond to this feedback.

6. Moderating panels: service users are involved in moderating placement portfolios, giving their views about the quality of evidence and decision making to the Examinations Board. There has been joint training arranged for service users, practitioners and university staff.

7. Selection: service users are involved as observers in the group interview and also play an equal part in individual interviews.

8. Overall, this involvement has been a developmental process for individual service users. They have been involved in a number of innovative activities such as giving papers at conferences and taking part in videos.

Practice example 2

University of Nottingham MA/Diploma in Social Work

Users' and Carers' Perspectives in Community Care

This module is designed, delivered and assessed by people who have all had contact with social work services as service users or as carers.

There is recognition that while community care legislation stresses the use of 'needs-led assessments', there is a history of and tendency for social workers to make decisions on behalf of service users.

The module attempts to redress the power imbalance between social workers and service users/carers. It does this by looking at the impact of social workers on people's lives and is directly informed by personal experience, ultimately proposing the rethinking of the nature of the relationship between social worker and service user and carer.

Learning methods: a number of people with direct experience of social work provide presentations throughout the module of their own experiences. The students are required to present their own life story to the whole group of students, academics and service users and carers, requiring the students to demonstrate their understanding of their own life pattern and development. This exercise in empathy is seen as a critical element in the social workers' ability to form a productive relationship with the service user. This experiential model requires the student to consider how service users and carers experience the world. They do this by listening to service users' and carers' personal experiences and considering the mechanisms by which service users and carers become oppressed.

During the telephone interviews and focus groups educators raised the following issues about partnership with service users and carers (from here on referred to collectively as 'service users').

a) 'Service user' is a contested term
Discussion on this point related to whether a 'service user' had to be someone currently receiving services. There were also concerns about whether some service users, particularly involuntary service users, were not being included in the partnership process. There were questions raised about whether students learned more from working with service users in practice settings rather than in the university. Another significant issue was the training of service users to take an equal part in partnership working, and whether this led inevitably to 'professionalisation'.

One educator summarised some of these dilemmas:

> I'd like to know what a service user is. It's a very simplistic definition. My colleague doesn't talk about service users. He talks about two categories, people who want to use services and people who don't want to use the services and we generally deal with people who want to use services or who have used the services and who no longer do. People with mental health difficulties who get better.... What we don't do very well, we don't engage with those people who don't want to engage with us or who we don't want to engage with.
> *(FGA 3)*

Educators and service users expressed contrasting views about the effectiveness of classroom involvement:

> Where students meet 'real' service users is in placement rather than college.

> What we have to ask is what is happening in practice because that is the opportunity students get to meet 'real' service users not ex-service users who are now part of some collaboration which is often what we get.
> *(TI)*

In contrast service users talked about introducing students to the 'real world' in the classroom:

> I see us as helping students with their course. We give information to students, in regard to the role-play. We are an introduction to the real world, and can result in better services to service users by social workers. We don't want to be criticised, talked to, and told off.
> *(FGSUC 4)*

b) Roles and responsibilities

Educators highlighted a range of issues that related to the quality of programme delivery, particularly in relation to service user involvement in learning, teaching and assessment. One module convenor referred to the 'horrendous responsibility' of convening a module where the staff had agreed user participation would be highlighted. Educators are attempting to clarify roles and responsibilities in a partnership model with, as one focus group discussed, the educator having primary responsibility for the outcome of student learning:

> Allowing them [user/carer] to have an input, which is useful for us. It's all very well talking partnership talk, but my profession, my employment is about training social workers and anything I do must be directed towards that aim. I'd like to do it in a way that is not damaging to any service user or carer or anybody else, the deal must be what's in it for me, not me but for what I'm trying to do.
> *(FGA)*

Or, as a programme director commented, this reflects an approach to stakeholder involvement, which is,

> Not just about service users but also about employers and practitioners. We are the people who are paid as educators therefore we are paid to do the work and we have taken the ideas to groups of stakeholders to discuss and get feedback.
> *(TI)*

Perhaps as an outcome of the above perspective, little data was found of users or carers taking direct responsibility for the design of learning, teaching or assessment where the view was that:

> We are taking responsibility for the bits we are experts in.
> *(TI)*

> I don't think, if we are honest, we don't have many, if any service users we are working with who are in tune enough with what we are trying to achieve that they would be involved with designing the course.
> *(TI)*

c) Teaching and learning in the classroom

Educators share some worries about the involvement of users and carers in learning, teaching and assessment, and the risks of what could be described as a personal testimony approach. At the beginning of the programme, listening to and learning from service user and carer experience was viewed as an important aspect of the learning. However, later in the programme, when analysis and a critical approach becomes more significant, the use of personal testimonies had limitations:

> We also need them [service users] to be more focused. [They] have experience of the mental health system but [they need to say] how it works and not leave the student to reflect and pick stuff up.
> *(TI)*

Educators attempt to address this by briefing service users to avoid them taking the agenda off in their own direction. This in itself requires a 'huge amount of time' and does not inevitably lead to the expected outcome:

> What we want someone to do and what they actually do on the day can be very different.
> *(TI)*

Educators also develop other teaching and learning approaches, such as one example among many where the educator took responsibility for linking theory and research while the service user brought their own perspective. This approach was not without its problems:

> We have to ensure that theory is dealt with elsewhere. That's a challenge and can end up in a split with boring lecturers and great service users.
> *(TI)*

Educators are also concerned that training, briefing and other activities designed to enhance partnership may result in the professionalisation of service users:

> The down side is if we attempt to train them up we lose the intrinsic value.
> *(FGA 3)*

d) Practical barriers

Educators are working to extend the range of user groups they partner with and increase their representativeness. Particular efforts were mentioned to involve young people and users from minority ethnic groups. They also have to manage a range of practical difficulties in partnering with service users in the classroom, many of which are addressed in the Levin (2004) study for SCIE of user and carer involvement. These include adapting hard-pressed university timetables to suit the timetable of service users; convincing university finance officers to adapt flexible payment systems; and difficulties of locating suitably accessible accommodation.

Issues of affordability are of ongoing concern. One module convenor in England talked about the dependence on the GSCC funding to justify service user participation in learning, teaching and assessment, as she felt sure that her university would not fund this activity when other academic staff were funded and available to teach.

Overall, as discussed later (section 3.4.5), activities to address these issues require the programme directors and the module convenors to find considerable time to resolve some of these dilemmas and encourage innovation.

Partnership of educator, social work student and other social work student

Student groups are extensively used in social work education and these are viewed as an excellent source of learning about partnership. The research included examples of working together in teaching, learning and assessment, students contributing to quality assurance processes as part of management groups and by providing feedback on specific modules.

In one focus group, students identified partnership working with other students as one of the most important aspects of learning:

> The group work is a good example of partnership. We have to work together and at the end of term we have to produce [an assessment] together. Also the learning sets where groups work together over two years.
> *(FGS 1)*

There is a well-established tradition of students contributing to learning, teaching and assessment by providing module or programme feedback. One educator commented on the significance of the process because it resulted in being part of change and development on the course:

> Generally student feedback is that they do believe their voices are heard and that they make a difference to the course.
> *(TI)*

One telephone interview specifically emphasised the importance of partnership work with students. Students were extensively involved in the programme, including student representatives participating in programme committees and ensuring effective communication with the total student group by disseminating material via the intranet and notice boards. The views of specific students were obtained through other group meetings such as the support group for black and minority ethnic students. (TI)

Educator, social work student and student from another profession

There is an increasing range of interprofessional modules, primarily with health professions, usually nursing, which may extend across programmes and academic levels. The following provide two examples:

- An Ethics and Professional Practice module involves teaching BA Social Work Year Two, MA Social Work Year One and post-qualified nurses. The emphasis of the module is how professionals work together in different contexts with different ethical issues and dilemmas (TI).
- A Multi-Professional Learning module is provided in all three years, becoming increasingly integrated as the course develops. Year One offers one session with a mixture of students from social work and nursing. Then the groups have separate teaching because of practicalities such as different placement patterns. In Year Two all teaching in the module is multiprofessional, exploring holistic assessment by looking at case studies to evaluate different professional contributions. All teaching groups are interprofessional and are taught and assessed interprofessionally.

Partnership of social work educator and educator from another profession

Partnership by social work educators with those from other professions may be conceptualised on a continuum. At one end is the social work educator who partners with an educator from another profession for one session, a shared learning event. Then there is partnering throughout one module, where there may be shared responsibility for convening and teaching the module. Practice example 6 provides an example of a Partnership and Participation module that is co-convened by Social Work and Nursing, and two seminar leaders are provided from each profession (for a total group of 80 students). There are other examples of interprofessional programmes where whole staff groups are interprofessional.

Partnership of educator, stakeholder and university

Programme directors view the learning, teaching and assessment of partnership as integrally linked to programme structures that include partnership features long associated with the DipSW. There is a strongly held view that such structures model partnership work. However, rarely is this conviction reflected in handbook documentation. An exception is the University of Wales Institute at Cardiff BA (Hons) Social Work programme handbook.

Practice example 3

University of Wales Institute at Cardiff BA (Hons) Social Work Programme

The 'programme philosophy' has two objectives including 'integration and collaboration', defined as 'through partnership and collaborative learning the Programme aims to integrate college and practice based learning ... principles of integration and collaboration, accessibility and flexibility are mainstreamed throughout the Programme in terms of management and organisation, selection and admission, structure and delivery, teaching, learning and assessment'.

The 12 educational aims of the programme include:

To build on and enhance the concept of partnership between agencies, the colleges, and users of social services.

The 'programme partnership' includes:

- 13 statutory and 2 voluntary sector agencies
- 2 service user and carer groups
- 2 Higher Education Institutions including a Further Education college.

Representatives of this form the Programme Management Committee. Sub-committees such as the Equal Opportunities

> Committee and the Allocation, Selection and Access Sub-Committee also include partner representatives.
>
> The programme director was clear about the importance of regularly auditing processes to ensure that integrated themes do not get lost or become something else over time.
>
> (BA Hons Social Work programme handbook 2004/05-2006/ 07, p 5)

A different example of structural partnerships is provided by another university, where the degree is designed and evaluated in partnership with an alliance (the old DipSW partners asked for the name to be changed to alliance rather than 'partnership'). This includes educators, students, user/carer groups, local authorities and a mental health trust. This strategic group forms a programme management group and several subgroups. It is involved in admissions. It is described as not being 'a top-down partnership' but engaging throughout the degree in a 'real' rather than 'tokenistic' way (TI).

3.4.4 What should partnership in social work education include, and how should it be included?

In this section the focus is on the content of learning, teaching and assessment and the methods used. The data identify two main approaches to this, conceptualised by the researchers as 'embedded and discrete'. In an 'embedded' approach, students learn by experiencing and/or observing partnership in different parts of the programme. In 'discrete' learning the knowledge, skills and/or values of partnership work are explicitly stated in learning aims and outcomes of a specific module and are assessed. A small number of programmes demonstrated both approaches.

The embedded approach to learning, teaching and assessing partnership

Here, the learning and teaching of partnership is integrated into other curriculum topics yet deliberately not made explicit. In a telephone interview, a programme director agreed that the word 'partnership' did not appear in the course documentation and indicated that the intention is to adopt an implicit approach to partnership learning by embedding it in the whole programme. An educator in another programme identified the advantages of this approach:

> Partnership teaching is embedded in other modules [two specific examples given]. Students should know, from the curriculum, the importance of partnership as theory, value and practice.
> *(TI)*

While another said:

> We don't teach partnership per se because we don't want it to be a bolt on.
> *(FGA 3)*

In the same programme the students said:

> We are taught about it all round, we don't think about it that much. Good practice is working with service users, getting feedback from people you are working with, anti-oppressive practice, person centred practice. It's in every social work method.
> *(FGS 3)*

Modelling partnership: linked to these ideas about partnership work pervading the course culture were comments about modelling good practice. In the following comments the 'modelling' of partnership is viewed as another source of learning about partnership:

> If the degree is not delivered in partnership then we are not providing a model of partnership for students. It is not just what you teach but how you teach it.
> *(TI)*

This may extend to learning in relation to individual modules. One educator described teaching a specific session with a service user as a specific example of modelling partnership (TI).

The infrastructure of practice learning was identified as another valuable resource for modelling partnership work:

> Partnership has to be modelled in the way in which placements are set up and run. In meetings between partners and students, practice teachers and college. Careful agreements and mid-term reviews must ensure that all the requirements in relation to partnership are covered.
> *(TI)*

Partnership across the curriculum: there were numerous examples provided of partnership learning from a range of other modules including Communication Skills and Law and Policy.

Communication Skills modules: communication skills were often cited as a location for students to learn how to work collaboratively with users and carers, including those with whom communication is difficult. Very specific skills might be needed, for example skills in negotiation and networking:

> New skill areas are developing. What used to be called boundary working in family therapy. Social workers need to lose their traditional defensiveness, their wish to extend their boundaries, 'only we are right' and because the key people are multi-skilled, have the skills at working across boundaries, negotiation and squaring the circles. This is difficult because people are driven to the certainty of tick boxes.
> *(FGA 3)*

One specific module focused on 'enhancing communication' with service users and with colleagues in other professions.

Law and Policy modules: much New Labour policy and related legislation is aimed at improving partnership working. Modules include sessions on these topics, which in turn then appear as an essay topic for an assessment task. For example, a Level One undergraduate Social Policy and Social Structure module, includes an essay title as follows:

Discuss the implications of 'partnership working' for the organisation and practice of social work.

At the University of Hull, partnership was included as part of a general introduction to social work.

Practice example 4

University of Hull MA Social Work

Introduction to Social Work Knowledge, Skills and Values

This module considers the context of contemporary social work practice and helps the student to understand new, integrated practice in the statutory and voluntary settings. In this module 'partnership' is embedded and implicit. Students are presented with an overview of contemporary models of social work assessment, particularly the Department of Health *Framework for Assessment*. This module considers the relation of different models of assessment to models of intervention and the skills required for social work practice: engagement, listening and communicating.

This module contains on opportunity to examine values in social work with particular attention to the GSCC Code of Practice and the BASW (British Association of Social Workers) Code of Ethics, in tandem with the concept of AOP.

The discrete approach to partnership learning, teaching and assessing partnership work

Variability of module content: an analysis of the content of nine modules about learning and teaching partnership work indicates that their focus is variable. Examples include modules that focus on organisations, ethical and AOP, the contested nature of social work and modules relating to particular service user and carer groups.

Comparison of module reading lists specifically about partnership suggests they also draw on a range of frameworks. The learning emphasis varies depending on the target audience but tends to focus on skill development (such as networking or communication), policy frameworks and organisational structures for developing interprofessional collaboration. There is a common emphasis on ethics, values and empowerment. In these specific modules the service user focus is evident from general texts and work in specific areas such as mental health, family group conferences and work with children and families.

In all the modules the lack of core texts is demonstrated by the diversity of material being sourced to support learning in this area of the university and practice curriculum, a matter reinforced by educators in telephone interviews and focus groups, and by students in focus groups.

Detailed examples of module content: the following are two very different modules which both demonstrate learning, teaching and assessment about partnership in different contexts.

Practice example 5

University of Bath BSc Social Work and Applied Social Sciences

Learning Partnership through Community Profiling

A community project combines college teaching with practice learning. The main outcome of the teaching and learning is completion of a community needs assessment.

Learning and teaching: university-based teaching includes learning how to gather information and then how to interpret and present it. Although these sources of learning are important, the main learning takes place in the community when students engage in research in partnership with people who are current or potential service users. Students undertake projects throughout the semester in small groups. These are provided with ongoing tutorial support. Each group presents a project during a session at the end of the semester. The aim is to present material in a coherent form that is useful information for the agencies who commissioned each project. The advantage for the agency is that they will have additional material to help improve services.

Assessment: students are assessed individually, on their groupwork and also their learning from the practice element of the project. Individual assessment consists of a written assignment that also contains an element of self-assessment. Students use learning logs, prior experience of similar work, discussion with group members as well as existing literature to develop a critical analysis of their learning from the project.

The group assessment consists of a project report that receives a single mark. Each report has to include a signed appendix that outlines the contribution made by each student.

Practice example 6

London South Bank University BA Level 2 Social Work and BSc Level 2 Nursing and Social Work Studies
Module: Partnership and Participation

This 10-week unit examines the core value of partnership within a context of health and social care practice. The unit explores the full range of partnership issues and contexts, looking at service user involvement, working with parents, working with families and carers and working in a community context. Interprofessional and interorganisational issues and practices are also investigated. In this way students are helped to identify and address issues associated with difference and to incorporate these understandings into their strategic thinking around boundaries and boundary crossings. The unit introduces students to some key issues and dilemmas and enables them to draw on a range of perspectives associated with partnership practice, with a particular focus on networking theories and methods.

The following views were expressed by social work students when asked about the main learning outcomes from the above Partnership and Participation module, shared with nursing students. They are quoted in full because they provide a summary of some of the issues about the concept and practice of partnership identified in the research. In a group led by a student researcher, the students said the following about the module:

Definitions and lack of theory

At the beginning we were given lots of definitions – lots of problems in language itself, you've got participation, inclusion, involvement.... At the beginning I found it very confusing.

[The lecturers talked] about the conceptual confusion and definitional problems of 'partnership' if you read one source one person will say that equals that, and if you read another they'll say, no that isn't that. So you've got all the contradictory literature that doesn't help.

In my personal opinion I did not find a great deal of real theory because in essence it's quite a simple philosophy. It is literally working in partnership you can't expand on it ... because you're working together, you're including your participating person.

Values

A lot of it is learning to communicate [with nursing students] but different professions will have different sets of values, like different jargon, so I do think to [it's important to] cover the areas of partnership.

When we had discussions right away you could see that we all had a different way of looking at things. You had to take on board what the other people came up with, you had to find kind of the middle line and straight away you were working in partnership because you couldn't get it your own way.

Skills, knowledge and process

I learnt a great deal about learning disability. The knowledge I gained from them made me feel a bit more confident if I am in that situation but also to me it typified the perfect partnership as we're using their expertise in that situation to help inform joint decisions.

A lot of it is learning to communicate really.

We were also lucky to have a module focused on language and communication and some of the skills and approaches we were looking were easily mapped into the partnership [module] and vice versa.... [It helped us to learn to] gain the trust to work in [partnership].

Partnership in practice

[They were asked about learning about partnership on placement and all agreed this learning had been valuable. However, they were quite critical of the 'partnership' practice they had observed.]

The partnership module has actually opened my eyes to the importance of involving everyone equally. Some people are more verbal than others but you try and make it equal opportunities for everyone to make the atmosphere such that everybody feels willing to participate. The module has helped my practice and [to] understand the importance of such issues.

It's brought awareness to me. I don't know that I didn't have it before, but it's definitely either fine-tuned it or given me more awareness of how these things work. How in multi-disciplinary meetings, it can be 'that's my view point' and 'that's my view point', and not really listening as much as possible to other people....There are so many different agencies and they're talking in their jargon.

Overall comments

It has given me so much insight.

Has been a very informative unit.

This course has helped me to see that I'm going to be in a position with power. That I need to be in a position where I feel confident enough to question whatever I feel I need to and is in the best interests of my client.

Teaching and learning methods

There are strong indications from the literature that adult learning methods may be particularly relevant to partnership learning, with its emphasis on participation and learning from each other. One example of a model that adopts an adult learning perspective uses problem-based learning in teaching about partnership.

Practice example 7

University of Sussex and University of Brighton BA Hons Social Work

Problem-based learning Partnership and Interprofessional Practice, Level One

Module aims: social work depends on partnership and collaboration with other professions. The central aim of this module is to study the theory and practice of such partnership and collaboration. It will be studied both in terms of the detail of the critical issues, good practice and the broader social and political context within which collaboration is sought. Issues of power and inequality in regard to 'race', class, disability and gender among others will be addressed throughout the module. Service users and practitioners will also make a contribution to teaching.

Learning methods: students are expected to be active learners and to work together during the module, learning about partnership and collaboration by reflecting on their own processes. The aim is that learning together will itself be helpful preparation for collaborative work in practice. A problem-based approach to learning will be used. Over the term, students will build their learning around a core case study about partnership and interprofessional practice in mental health.

Weekly pattern: each day will begin with a whole group lecture. While this session is based around a lecture format, discussions and various exercises will also play a part. The second part of the morning and afternoon sessions will involve work in study groups. The morning study group will be held with a facilitator; the afternoon group will be student led. Staff facilitators will enable the group to focus on learning from the module content and also from group process.

Case scenario: the students work on a detailed scenario that focuses on partnership working in mental health. The students are also provided with a reading list that directs them to general themes and specific material related to the scenario:

Partnership and Interprofessional Practice

Assessed Group Presentation, 9 June 2005

Markers' Comment Sheet

The presentation will be marked out of 30. Each of the following five criteria will be equally weighted with up to six marks allocated to each:

1. How well do the group demonstrate an initial awareness of the use of theories or research in understanding interprofessional practice and the Joe Jacobs scenario?
2. How well do the group demonstrate an initial understanding of the differing and potentially conflicting perspectives of different professionals and agencies and their implications for successful intervention to support Joe?
3. How well do the group demonstrate an initial understanding of interprofessional partnership with users and carers of people with mental health problems?
4. How well is the group able to evaluate collaboration by the study group in preparation for the presentation?
5. How does the overall presentation demonstrate coherence (including time management), accessibility and creativity?

There were other examples of using a range of experiential and interactive learning approaches including learning logs and making and using videos. A particularly innovative example at London Metropolitan University requires the setting up of simulated conferences to involve different stakeholders in the learning process.

Practice example 8

London Metropolitan University BA Social Work

The Use of Conferences

Partnership Working and Management

In this module, the participation in an interprofessional conference forms part of the assessment of the student's work.

The conference is simulated, with the students playing various roles, based on a real case. The aim of the conference is to demonstrate key aspects of partnership working. The student must demonstrate key attributes of interprofessional working: communication, decision making and recognition of power imbalances. The students are observed by a panel of service users and carers who give feedback to the student on their performance.

Other educators are developing learning tools that present the user perspective through the use of videos rather than 'parachuting in' users and carers, or by using literature:

The impact of the user view is already there centrally in the literature and what is said in that is so much better than what you would get by inviting somebody who is inexperienced to come and deliver something in the classroom.
(TI)

A combined embedded and discrete approach to learning, teaching and assessing partnership work

In interviews and focus groups there was a small group of educators who identified providing discrete modules embedded in a programme where the philosophy of partnership and the structures that reflect this pervade the whole programme. These tend to be the courses where the research team sought (not always successfully) to arrange focus groups.

Learning about partnership work in practice

There is an assumption that students learn about partnership work in practice. Yet, as one educator commented:

We don't know to what extent that way of [partnership] working is really being taught.
(TI)

There is also a view that partnership work may not be common in practice:

> I do think it's happening but don't think it's happening fast enough. It's coming but it's taking a long time to happen.
> *(FGS 3)*

The absence of 'partnership' work in the England NOS combines with a lack of agreement and clarity about what partnership work entails:

> When students arrive in placement they have differing levels and range of understanding of the term partnership. Often used as a misnomer, it's a very broad general term that can mean lots of different things to different people and groups. In micro-form it would involve a true partnership working alongside each other but in reality there are unequal and uncomfortable relationships between service users and the establishment to some degree. We try to extend a student's view of partnership to think more laterally because some partnerships do have a financial relationship.
> *(FGP 1)*

Such comments highlight the need for a partnership curriculum. Of the respondents we spoke to no one had a practice curriculum that specified partnership work but there are various methods of monitoring that partnership work is being learnt and assessed, for example, the widespread use of practice portfolios. Not all of these specifically assess partnership work but rather accessed it through other requirements, for example, case studies and the direct observation of practice (TI).

There is a common view among educators and students that 'the field' is behind on the partnership issue. As this focus group of educators and practitioners said:

> Partnership working is essential but practice assessors and practitioners still think about this concept in the way they did when they were trained. They have not moved on.
> *(FGA 1)*

There is a serendipitous aspect as to whether students will or will not learn partnership work in practice settings. Another focus group of educators made the following comments:

> The problem with practice is that the setting will determine the skills you get from it. No matter how you slice it, places like social service departments are insular and no matter what artificialities you put on it any close examination will show that they are moving away from a notion of partnership. There are a number of reasons for this – specialisation, managerialism, bureaucracy – and partnership in whatever form becomes more and more a bolt on. Even the notion of what I would call programme-orientated organisations such as Youth Offending Teams are not partnership at all.... Other newer organisations are looking at things in a new light and have a better idea as to how to do this.... I'm thinking of things like Sure Start.
> *(FGA 3)*

A student, from a different programme, endorsed the above viewpoint:

> It's such a shock when you go out on placement. You've got the theory but they're not into theory, they're into workloads, budgets and we're like you're not talking about theory. They do go by theory but it's not a priority whereas we go by the ideals, this approach, legislation, and this theory – they don't think like that. It's how to handle your caseload, different types of questioning. In lectures we do case scenarios but it's not the same as going out to a service user's house on your own, where they don't know about communication skills. We have to adapt to their level.
> *(FGS 1)*

Educators are concerned about an anti-partnership sentiment in some areas of practice:

> From reading students' work I think that what is being taught is that service users are the enemy.
> *(TI)*

An example was provided of a student in a mental health setting where the 'service user' meant a person who uses up the budget and makes life difficult for those who are working there:

> So we meet all kinds of canteen culture. Sometimes we have students who are astute and who can learn despite that. Other times we have students we worry about because we see them moving into the culture.
> *(TI)*

Educators also expressed concern about student resistance to being placed in non-traditional agencies where there might be enhanced opportunity for learning about partnership but there might not be any social workers:

> The big issue is the way students perceive interprofessional learning in practice. At the end of last year there was a meeting with the employment-based students who were concerned about not being assessed by a social worker. At that time we were talking very positively about learning in different professional environments, the diversity of placements. I think [the students'] view is a very justifiable one to take. If I'm training to be a social worker shouldn't I be assessed by a social worker, shouldn't I be supervised by a social worker, shouldn't I be working in a social work environment? Otherwise, how do I know that what I am learning is social work?
> *(TI)*

One programme offered a placement in a voluntary organisation which had been contracted by the local authority to manage Direct Payments and which provided opportunities to meet the NOS. Students were reluctant to use the placement as they would not be working in a social work office. There was awareness that students needed more information and placement preparation:

> Where our [the course] learning needs to be focused is certainly around trying to move students away from the notion that they have to be in a particular organisation in order to be doing social work and anywhere else they are not.
> *(TI)*

Another programme linked 'resistance' of this kind to lack of knowledge. They arranged a university-based meeting to disseminate information about non-traditional practice learning opportunities. The meeting was attended by current students, students placed in non-traditional settings, local organisations and practice learning organisers (TI).

Views were also expressed by educators and practitioners that non-traditional and partnership placements would soon become the norm.

A programme director reflected on which would come first, changing organisations or changing practice? Practitioners in the same university thought that partnership work was inevitable as practice moves towards integrated service provision:

> It will almost happen automatically, this will be the driver.
> *(FGP 1)*

3.4.5 When should partnership in social work education take place?

Timing and staging

Linked with the issue of providing a module about partnership and/or embedding it in the curriculum is the question of the timing and staging of learning about partnership.

Arguments were commonly made by respondents that students should learn about partnership with service users and carers from very early in the programme, as this sets the context for embedding the philosophy about working with users and carers.

In Site 3 the educators reported their conviction about the importance of early learning about partnership and their view was echoed in the student focus group. The students reported that they had been told when they started the course that service users had been involved in the planning. These students had a 30-day placement in the first year that included a community development project. The students regarded this as an example of good partnership practice as small groups worked with agencies in the voluntary and independent sector on a project identified by service users (FGS 3).

Students who have participated in this kind of approach early in their programme have not yet reached qualifying level and are unable to comment yet on whether it has been sustained.

Time available to learn, teach and assess partnership work

A theme that recurred in the telephone interviews and the focus groups was that the learning, teaching and assessment of partnership work requires time if it is to be effective. Time is required for key 'actors' to get to know each other, to learn to work together and to trust each other. Time may be required for training, for example, for service users and carers to participate effectively. Practice across boundaries is innovative and innovation requires time to plan and to engage stakeholders. Crucially time is necessary to develop and sustain partnership work with users and carers and to avoid tokenism. A service user group identified that if teaching sessions involving stakeholders are to be effective, they take more time than anticipated to prepare and plan and that joint planning of the sessions is essential to avoid the process of 'being parachuted in'.

3.4.6 How do partners benefit?

Benefits for service users and carers

The research team found that users and carers were keen to discuss what they gain from partnership working. Service users and carers are paid to participate – although payment systems, as discussed elsewhere (Levin, 2004), are contested. Payment is not presented as a key reason to participate. Rather there appear to be two main groups of reasons for users and carers to work in partnership with programmes:

Users and carers gain what might be identified as 'therapeutic' value:

- A group of service users discussed their reasons for being involved with the course and described how it gave individuals something to do. It increased confidence and self-esteem, knowledge and skills, including assessment skills, as a result of giving presentations at conferences, being part of video presentations, being involved in different aspects of assessment. The process was one of collective and individual capacity building (FGSU 3).

- At Site 4, a group of service users and carers talked about the value of involvement for self-esteem, and for turning a negative experience into a positive one. For carers it reduced their isolation.

In at least three programmes in the study service users and carers are provided with the opportunity to obtain accreditation for their participation.

- A group of service users with learning difficulties give a presentation on selection days. The material they present focuses on a topic chosen by them, for example, what makes a good social worker? They are paid but they also receive credit as part of vocational training. The aim in future is to extend this model, which has been well received by candidates, to other service user groups.
- Service users are offered the opportunity at another university to participate in an accredited short course, 'Training the trainers'.

Benefits for practitioners

The new degrees and the emphasis on partnership working may be infusing some new life into partnership work with practitioners:

One university described a new development, which involves an agreement with local agencies to enable experienced members of staff to become involved in teaching. With the consent of their managers they will be involved with teaching and assessing a module on reflective practice. They no longer have to take leave and be paid as a sessional teacher and this work will be regarded as a contribution to Continuing Professional Development.

Key findings and conclusions

4.1 Reflections on methodology

4.1.1 Reflections on the Research Review methodology

Quality of the data extracted studies

There are limits to the overall weight to be given to some of the data extracted studies. Most measured changes in attitudes following, or during and immediately after, course participation, without follow-up into practice. Only Whittington and Bell (2001) followed students through a year into practice, and Fineberg et al (2004) included a three-month follow-up. Many acknowledged this as a limitation of their studies. Furthermore, they acknowledged that changes in attitudes are not necessarily indicative of subsequent behaviour. The timing of measurements taken to establish effectiveness is crucial here, since changes might take longer to influence attitudes, beliefs and subsequent behaviour. Likewise, early signs of change might not be sustained in the longer term.

Six of the data extracted studies rely on single sources of data. Given that two of these studies are wholly qualitative and two others partly so, establishing greater trustworthiness through triangulating data from multiple sources might have been anticipated to be a characteristic of these studies, but it was not generally the case. Reporting of the studies was highly variable and as with other experiences of systematic reviewing, abstracts gave too little specific detail in many cases to judge whether or not the study was relevant to the review.

Samples

Data extracted studies that addressed partnership with users and carers were undertaken exclusively in social work education contexts. However, predictably, the studies of interprofessional education were often in multidisciplinary contexts, mainly health and social work with one study on law and social work students. The number of social workers in those studies using multiprofessional samples was low compared to the proportion of other professional groups. For example, in the Kane (1976) study there were just three social workers in the sample and in Pollard et al (2006) just 3.6% of the overall sample, making it very difficult to extrapolate broader findings to the social workers in particular.

Reviewing process

The process of selection of studies for inclusion in the data extraction seems to have favoured interprofessional education over other types of partnership. This may reflect the nature of the studies, with those in the user participation area involving more exploratory work with small groups. However, the same predominant interprofessional partnership focus was reflected in the wider review, suggesting either just more published work on interprofessional partnership, or more education initiatives to report, or both.

The keywording system and data extraction tools developed by the EPPI-Centre were unsuitable in their existing forms for applications to social work literature. For example, the questions referred to pupils, schools and school subjects and did not refer to service users, practice teachers or social work agencies. This set a considerable methodological challenge in the first few months of the project when unplanned-for time had to be allocated to development work. However, the tools developed for this review may be adaptable for other reviews relating to social work and social care contexts.

This the first time that the EPPI-Centre systematic review methodology has been used for reviewing social work topics. The methodology has clear advantages, allowing mapping and data extraction across the full range of research methodologies. On the basis of this experience, it will be helpful to complement the systematic approach to assessing empirical methodology with equally rigorous scrutiny of conceptual and descriptive content.

4.1.2 Reflections on the Practice Survey methodology

The Practice Survey examined rather than evaluated current practice. The data from programme handbooks proved very mixed, and although it served to demonstrate that 'partnership' as a theme is largely invisible, it was not useful in mapping the territory. In contrast, the examination of module handbooks, particularly in conjunction with telephone interviews with module convenors, was a rich source of data. Similarly focus groups provided rich data.

The research team was interdisciplinary including academics from three different disciplines, a practitioner-researcher and an early career research assistant. The team worked effectively in partnership, assisted by being co-located and having a core of prior established working relationships. The strategy to involve users and carers and students as co-researchers informed research team practice. The partnership with the EPPI-Centre proved a good source of learning.

4.2 Key findings

4.2.1 Key findings from the Research Review

Clarity of definition

Conceptual confusion about partnership is rife in the social work educational research literature. The concept is under-theorised, simultaneously contested and taken for granted (for example, Jackson and Morris, 1994; Julia and Kondrat, 2000). There is no guarantee that greater clarity would lead to better practice. However, on the basis of this Review, we would argue that judgements about the effectiveness of partnership work education might more easily be made if the concept is clarified and developed.

Who is involved in partnership?

The majority of studies in the Review focus on interprofessional partnership work, involving predominantly health-related professions (for example, nursing, occupational therapy, speech therapy, midwifery and general practice) with law and education only occasionally mentioned. The empirical studies show no significant differences in outcomes with, or for, different professional groups. However, there is some evidence (for example, Whittington and Bell, 2001) that social work students perceived particular professional groups, such as nurses, as having a better understanding of social work roles than did those, such as doctors and police, with whom they often need to work, but rarely train.

Partnership with users and carers in social work education includes children and families, mental health, disability, child protection and other areas of practice; there seems no less attention paid to partnership in areas that may involve some degree of social control (such as mental health or child protection) than others. This said, the important question of how to think about, let alone address the particular challenges of working in partnership with those who do not want to participate is rarely raised in the education literature.

What does partnership involve and how is it done?

The majority of partnership education initiatives reviewed involve discrete modules, or projects, where, typically, students of different professions worked together towards shared goals, or users brought their own experiences to the classroom. Rarer were those initiatives reported where partnership work could be described as embedded throughout programme curricula, structures and processes. The most far-reaching such examples for interprofessional partnership work were integrated joint programmes, with students from different professions learning together throughout. The complexities of providing such programmes have been highlighted, but none has been rigorously evaluated (Barr and Waterton, 1996a, 1996b).

There are a few impressive examples reported of partnership with users and carers in social work education, including the new degree programmes at the Universities of Plymouth and Dundee (Ager et al, 2005; Elliott et al, 2005). These developments need strong institutional support, motivation, establishment of strong grassroots networks, careful attention to practicalities and principals; they tend to rest firmly on a value-based commitment to partnership.

Many of the discrete partnership education initiatives reported demonstrate the type of 'creative and inclusive methods of promoting partnership' called for by Levin (2004) on behalf of SCIE. They focus on students developing understanding of other professions and intergroup relations, on distinctions and commonalities in core knowledges and value bases, and on the development of collaborative, communication, networking and conflict resolution skills (Barr and Waterton, 1996a, 1996b).

There is an increasing number of examples in the literature of user and carer participation in teaching about partnership work, either, to use Manthorpe's (2000) distinction, as co-trainers, or as bearers of the testimony of their own experience. The emphasis here is on developing students' understandings, empathy and interpersonal skills, reducing stereotypes, and recognising users' and carers' strengths and identities. Two of the data extracted studies evaluated specific examples, one involving parents of children with disabilities (Wikler, 1979) and the other, users of mental health services (Scheyett and Kim, 2004). They suggest that a model of consumer-partnered social work education using structured dialogue, acknowledges the wisdom and experience of service users and enables them to become fully engaged in teaching, assessment, course review and curriculum committees that will shape future social workers.

Some studies (for example, Jackson and Morris, 1994) suggest practice learning as a better opportunity for learning about partnership than taught modules. The process of setting up the placement itself was seen as an opportunity to model partnership between student, tutor and practice teacher, although students noted the power differentials that sometimes limited their involvement.

Several papers make the case for user involvement in the assessment of student practice, arguing that this empowers consumers and can provide a valuable source of feedback for students. This requires time and resources, attention to confidentiality and representation, avoidance of tokenism, and the ability to disaggregate service issues from student practice. There is scope for development in this area; as yet, despite some innovative initiatives, most user/carer assessment of students is indirect and informal.

Coverage of the implications of 'race', class, sexuality, religion, culture and language was not prominent. Jackson and Morris (1994) report that 'race' and language were better addressed than the other areas, in the education programmes that they examined, but argue that if there is little explicit teaching in all these areas, an understanding of how oppression can create barriers to partnership working will not be grasped.

When should partnership take place?

The timing of interprofessional partnership learning is contested, with the issue linked to concerns about the establishment and consolidation of professional identity and confidence. Glen (2001) advocates interprofessional learning before boundaries and stereotypes have become entrenched; however, she and others (for example, Johnson, 2003) warn against the dilution of professional skills where an interprofessional priority is adopted early. Kane (1976) suggests that the key is to combine understandings but contribute separate talents, and many studies contest that the issue is less about *when* it happens and more about the tensions created to *fit it all in*.

From rhetoric to reality – what works?

There are no overall conclusive findings reported on whether partnership work in social work education is effective for students, nor which approaches to teaching and learning about partnership might be more effective than others. This is particularly so since only two of the studies reviewed in-depth followed students through into subsequent practice, and one of these did so only three months after qualification. Where reports claim that partnership education has been effective, they focus mainly on student perspectives, attitudes and knowledge, not on demonstration of practice as such. Even here, there are mixed findings. The Pollard et al (2006: forthcoming) survey provides a large-scale study within which there are variable findings about perceptions of interprofessional work; likewise the other studies addressing effectiveness are characterised by mixed or indicative, rather than secure, results.

However, some messages do emerge about the factors that support partnership, such as making clear and reiterating the definition and expectations of partnership, making greater use of practice learning to promote partnership, developing more extensive and integrated user and carer participation, modelling partnership through interdisciplinary provider teams, establishing partnership-based relationships with students, and possibly (although this remains the subject of debate) introducing interprofessional experiences earlier into the social work education process.

Studies rarely claim to tell us whether partnership education improves service outcomes for consumers. However, there seems good evidence that, if well managed, the process itself can be valuable for users and carers. Scheyett and Kim, for example, suggest that the 'structured dialogue' partnership model they describe honours service users' and carers' experience and wisdom by inviting them to participate in the education process. In this sense 'a school of social work can model for students true partnership with consumers in a strengths-based framework' (Scheyett and Kim, 2004, p 51). This would seem to be an appropriate aim emerging from this Review.

Overall, the evidence predictably suggests rather greater commitment to education for partnership work with users and carers, and between professionals, than the outcome evidence from research can sustain at this time. However, this partly reflects the nature of the available evidence base rather than the state of education, the impacts of which remain largely undetected and unidentified. The implementation of partnership-focused education needs more research that evaluates longer-term effects and monitors changes for the same population over time using multiple sources or more carefully designed comparative studies.

Glen (2001) and others remind us that interprofessional education is driven predominantly by a policy agenda, and that issues of cost-effectiveness that might be priorities for national policy or local providers are sometimes in conflict with the professional commitment to partnership. Partnership with users and carers, in contrast, is driven largely by an empowerment agenda. These influences will need to be taken into account in determining who undertakes the research and whose perspectives are included.

4.2.2 Key findings from the Practice Survey

Professional culture and identity

A specific research objective in relation to exploring the impact of issues of professional culture and identity on social work education had not been identified in the Review proposal. However, this issue emerged as significant and it seems likely that this will be reinforced by the pending Knowledge Review of Interprofessional Education [to be conducted in 2006]. Throughout the Practice Survey, questions arose with all stakeholders about the value of different kinds of expertise and knowledge and the challenges of learning to deal with differences and work across boundaries. This raises questions identified by Trevillion and Bedford (2003). Is partnership working about 'pragmatism' and learning how to work together with others where the ideals can only be validated in relation to practice? Or, is partnership about 'utopianism', learning how to be a flexible and holistic practitioner, preparing new kinds of practitioners for a better future world? Is it about the pragmatic response as this practitioner identified in the Practice Survey?

> It's not about saying I'm a social worker and I can only do this and I'm a nurse and I can only do this, because that's what service users tell us that they don't want, to see 20 people between going into hospital and going out.... Equally, we don't want student social workers who think they are all things to all people and trying to do everything single handedly. What we try to do is say these are service cases ... corporate ownership in the organisation.
> *(Lancs Practitioners FG)*

Or, alternatively, is it the utopian response as expressed by this programme director?

> Do we need not only a different kind of worker but different organisation? The' full logic' of partnership will result in new organisations.
> *(TI)*

Defining and clarifying the concept of partnership work

The requirement for partnership working is implicit rather than explicit in the NOS, although it is specifically required in parts of the regulatory requirements of Wales and Northern Ireland. The Practice Survey found that partnership working was also implicit rather than explicit in course documentation. It is regarded as self-evident that partnership will be central to the learning, possibly because it is a value to which everyone can subscribe.

Partnership is not clearly defined. It is a broad and complex concept most frequently associated with work with service users and carers or work with other professionals. It is also a contested concept viewed very differently by different providers and also by different parts of the same system.

Links between partnership work and anti-oppressive work

Several participants identified similarities between education for partnership and education for AOP. This was expressed in a number of ways: AOP is the core of effective partnership working, partnership is about managing power, it requires constant attention and is always 'work in progress'.

Partnership structures and how partnership work is addressed

Like the Research Review, the Practice Survey confirmed that the concept of partnership is under-theorised. Underpinning knowledge draws on a range of related material including organisation and empowerment theory. There is a lack of core texts on which to draw.

The Practice Survey identifies a number of interacting relationships that make up the fabric of partnership education. These include service users and carers, educators, practitioners, students and other professionals. The greater emphasis on service user and carer involvement in the new degree means that this aspect of partnership receives particular attention.

There appear to be three main approaches to partnership structures and curriculum: the embedded educational model, the discrete model and a combined approach. Each approach has a clearly articulated rationale and there is evidence of good practice examples of each identified in the research.

Partnership work in practice learning

In practice learning no examples of a defined 'partnership curriculum' were identified. The findings on partnership in practice learning are contradictory and frequently appear to depend on the commitment of individual organisations and practitioners. Some participants argue that practice is the 'driver' for partnership education since policy requires joint working and service user involvement. Others feel that the university curriculum is determining the quality of partnership learning and practice is following or even lagging behind.

When partnership work is addressed

Time itself was found to be an important aspect of developing effective partnership education. This includes both the time involved in developing and maintaining relationships and also the timing and staging of teaching and learning about partnership. In the literature, there is considerable debate about the timing of interprofessional learning, particularly in terms of the development of professional identity. There is no similar debate about the timing of service user involvement. There is agreement that this should happen as early as possible, both in course planning and delivery.

Programmes are involved in micro-evaluations of partnership teaching and learning. More extensive evaluation, focused on some of the initiatives developed for the new degree, will be required to explore the relationships between identified aims and outcomes and the development of good practice.

References

Included in data extraction

Carpenter, J. and Hewstone, M. (1996) 'Shared learning for doctors and social workers: evaluation of a programme', *British Journal of Social Work*, vol 26, no 2, pp 239-57.

Colarossi, L. and Forgey, M.A. (2006) 'Evaluation study of an interdisciplinary social work and law curriculum for domestic violence', *Journal of Social Work Education*, vol 42, no 2, pp 371-387.

Fineberg, I.C., Wenger, N.S. and Forrow, L. (2004) 'Interdisciplinary education: evaluation of a palliative care training intervention for pre-professionals', *Academic Medicine*, vol 79, no 8, pp 769-76.

Hyer, K., Fairchild, S., Abraham, I., Mezey, M. and Fulmer, T. (2000) 'Measuring attitudes related to interdisciplinary training: revisiting the Heinemann, Schmitt and Farrell "attitudes toward health care teams' scale", *Journal of Interprofessional Care*, vol 14, no 3, pp 249-58.

Jackson, S. and Morris, K. (1994) *Looking at Partnership Teaching in Social Work Qualifying Programmes*, London: CCETSW.

Johnson, R. (2003) 'Exploring students' views of interprofessional education', including commentary by S. Reeves and J. Kennard, *International Journal of Therapy and Rehabilitation*, vol 10, no 7, pp 314-20.

Julia, M. and Kondrat, M.E. (2000) 'Participatory action research and MSW curricula: are social work research courses meeting the challenge?', *Journal of Teaching in Social Work*, vol 20, nos 3-4, pp 101-24.

Kane, R.A. (1976) 'Interprofessional education and social work: a survey', *Social Work in Health Care*, vol 2, no 2, pp 229-38.

Pollard, K.C., Miers, M.E. and Gillchrist, M. (2006: forthcoming) 'Second year scepticism: pre-qualifying health and social care students' midpoint self-assessment, attitudes and perceptions concerning interprofessional learning and working', *Journal of Interprofessional Care*.

Scheyett, A. and Kim, M. (2004) '"Can we talk?": using facilitated dialogue to positively change student attitudes towards persons with mental illness', *Journal of Teaching in Social Work*, vol 24, nos 1-2, pp 39-54.

Shor, R. and Sykes, I.J. (2002) 'Introducing structured dialogue with people with mental illness into the training of social work students', *Psychiatric Rehabilitation Journal*, vol 26, no 1, pp 63-9.

Whittington, C. and Bell, L. (2001) 'Learning for interprofessional and inter-agency practice in the new social work curriculum: evidence from an earlier research study', *Journal of Interprofessional Care*, vol 15, no 2, pp 153-69.

Wikler, L. (1979) 'Consumer involvement in the training of social work students', *Social Casework*, vol 60, no 3, pp 145-9.

Included in research review

Ager, W., Dow, J. and Gee. M. (2005) 'A model for promoting the influence of service users and carers in social work education', *Social Work Education*, vol 24, no 4, pp 467-76.

Alsop, A. and Vigars, C. (1996) *Shared Learning, Joint Training or Dual Qualification for Occupational Therapy and Social Work: Report of a Feasibility Study for CCETSW*, London: CCETSW.

Atkins, J.M. and Walsh, R.S. (1997) 'Developing shared learning in multiprofessional health care education: for whose benefit?', *Nurse Education Today*, vol 17, no 4, pp 319-24.

Barr, H. (1996) 'Ends and means in interprofessional education: towards a typology', *Education for Health: Change in Learning & Practice*, vol 9, pp 341-52.

Barr. H. and Waterton, S. (1996a) *Interprofessional Education in Health and Social Care in the United Kingdom. Report of a CAIPE Survey*, London: CAIPE.

Barr. H. and Waterton, S. (1996b) 'Summary of a CAIPE survey: interprofessional education in health and social care in the United Kingdom', *Journal of Interprofessional Care*, vol 10, no 3, pp 297-305.

Barr, H., Freeth, D., Hammick, M., Koppel, I. and Reeves, S. (2000) *Evaluations of Interprofessional Education: A United Kingdom Review for Health and Social Care*, London: CAIPE/British Educational Research Association.

Beresford, P. (1994) *Changing the Culture: Involving Service Users in Social Work Education*, London: CCETSW.

Bordelon, T.D. (2003) 'People first: a case study in partnering with the community', *The Journal of Baccalaureate Social Work*, vol 8, no 2, pp 147-61.

Boylan, J., Dalrymple, J. and Ing, P. (2000) 'Let's do it! Advocacy, young people and social work education', *Social Work Education*, vol 19, no 6, pp 553-63.

Brandon, R.N. and Knapp, M.S. (1999) 'Interprofessional education and training: transforming professional preparation to transform human services', *American Behavioral Scientist*, vol 42, no 5, pp 876-91.

Brown, G.M. (1990) 'The teaching case conference as a method of practice education and training', *Social Work Education*, vol 9, no 1, pp 24-34.

Burns, C., Smith, A., Hyer, K., Jacobson, H., Lowry, L., Reed, C. and Westhoff, W. (2000) 'Training the interdisciplinary team in primary care', *National Academies of Practice Forum*, vol 2, no 2, pp 95-100.

Chartier, L., Pronovost, L., Malavoy, M. and Jinchereau, F. (1984) 'An experiment in interdisciplinary education', *Canadian Nurse*, vol 80, no 7, pp 10-11.

Citizens as Trainers Group, Rimmer, A. and Harwood, K. (2004) 'Citizen participation in the education and training of social workers', *Social Work Education*, vol 23, no 3, pp 309-23.

Connolly, P.M. and Novak, J.M. (2000) 'Teaching collaboration: a demonstration model', *Journal of the American Psychiatric Nurses Association*, vol 6, no 6, pp 183-90.

Cook, A., Davis, J. and Vanclay, L. (2001) 'Shared learning in practice placements for health and social work students in East London: a feasibility study', *Journal of Interprofessional Care*, vol 15, no 2, pp 185-90.

Cuming, H. and Wilkins, J. (2000) 'Involving service users in the assessment of students in professional practice', *Journal of Practice Teaching in Social Work and Health*, vol 3, no 2, pp 17-30.

Curran, T. (1997) 'Power, participation and post-modernism: user and practitioners participation in mental health social work education', *Social Work Education*, vol 16, no 3, pp 21-36.

Damon-Rodriguez, J. and Corley, C.S. (2002) 'Social work education for interdisciplinary practice with older adults and their families', *Journal of Gerontological Social Work*, vol 39, nos 1-2, pp 37-55.

Edwards, C. (2003) 'The involvement of service users in the assessment of Diploma in Social Work students on practice placements', *Social Work Education*, vol 22, no 4, pp 341-9.

Elliott, T., Frazer, T., Farrard, D., Hickinbotham, J., Horton, V., Mann, J., Soper, S., Turner, J., Turner, M. and Whiteford, A. (2005) 'Practice learning and assessment on BSc (Hons) Social Work: "Service user conversations"', *Social Work Education*, vol 24, no 4, pp 451-66.

Etchells, E. and Kniveton, K. (2000) 'The Salford and Manchester experience of developing and enabling learning for partnership working', in CCETSW (ed) *Preparing Qualifying Social Workers for Interprofessional Working. Friday 8th September 2000: Workshop Report*, London: CCETSW.

Etchells, J., Kniveton, K., Longshaw, K. and Mitchell, D. (1999) 'Dual qualification education and training: the learning disability experience', *Mental Health Care*, vol 2, no 12, pp 412-15.

Flaherty, E., Hyer, K., Kane, R., Wilson, N., Whitelaw, N. and Fulmer, T. (2003) 'Using case studies to evaluate students' ability to develop a geriatric interdisciplinary care plan', *Gerontology & Geriatrics Education*, vol 24, no 2, pp 63-74.

Glen, S. (2001) 'Transdisciplinary education: tensions and contradictions?', *Nursing Times Research*, vol 6, no 5, pp 807-16.

Gonzales, D.B., Gangluff, D.L. and Eaton, B.B. (2004) 'Promoting family-centred, interprofessional health education through the use of solution-focused learning', *Journal of Interprofessional Care*, vol 18, no 3, pp 317-19.

Gronski, R. and Pigg, K. (2000) 'University and community collaboration: experiential learning in human services', *American Behavioral Scientist*, vol 43, no 5, pp 781-92.

Grossman, B. and McCormick, K. (2003) 'Preparing social work students for interdisciplinary practice: learnings from a curriculum development project', *Journal of Human Behavior in the Social Environment*, vol 7, nos 1/2, pp 97-113.

Hammick, M. (2000) 'Interprofessional education: evidence from the past to guide the future', *Medical Teacher: An International Journal of Education in Practice for Educators in the Health Sciences*, vol 22, no 5, pp 461-7.

Heinemann, G.D., Scmidt, M.H., Farrell, M.P. and Brailler, S.A. (1999) 'Development of an Attitudes Toward Health Care Teams Scale,' *Evaluation and the Health Professions*, vol 22, no 1, pp 123-142.

Henderson, J. (1994) 'Reflecting oppression: symmetrical experiences of social work students and service users', *Social Work Education*, vol 13, pp 16-25.

Hendricks, C.O. and Rudich, G. (2000) 'A community building perspective in social work education', *Journal of Community Practice*, vol 8, no 3, pp 21-36.

Hewstone, M., Carpenter, J., Franklyn-Stokes, A. and Routh, D. (1994) 'Intergroup contact between professional groups: two evaluation studies', *Journal of Community & Applied Social Psychology*, vol 4, pp 347-63.

Huff, M.T. and Johnson, M.M. (1998) 'Empowering students in a graduate-level social work course', *Journal of Social Work Education*, vol 34, no 3, pp 375-85.

Humphris, D. and Hean, S. (2004) 'Educating the future workforce: building the evidence about interprofessional learning', *Journal of Health Services Research & Policy*, vol 9, Supplement 1, pp 24-7.

Jivanjee, P.R. and Friesen, B.J. (1997) 'Shared expertise: family participation in interprofessional training', *Journal of Emotional and Behavioral Disorders*, vol 5, no 4, pp 205-11.

Johnston, G. and Banks, S. (2000) 'Interprofessional learning modules at Dalhousie University', *The Journal of Health Administration Education*, vol 18, no 4, pp 407-27.

Kacen, L. (1998) 'Intergroup bridging using the Dynamic Circles Exercise (DCE)', *Simulation and Gaming*, vol 29, no 1, pp 88-100.

Karban, K. (2003) 'Social work education and mental health in a changing world', *Social Work Education*, vol 22, no 2, pp 191-202.

Koppel, I., Barr, H., Reeves, S., Freeth, D. and Hammick, M. (2001) 'Establishing a systematic approach to evaluating the effectiveness of interprofessional education', *Issues in Interdisciplinary Care*, vol 3, no 1, pp 41-9.

Lough, M.A., Schmidt, K. and Leshan, L. (1999) 'An interdisciplinary service learning program promotes collaborative health care', *National Academies of Practice Forum: Issues in Interdisciplinary Care*, vol 1, no 4, pp 255-61.

Lough, M.A., Schmidt, K., Swain, G.R., Naughton, T.M., Leshan, L.A., Blackburn, J.A. and Mancuso, P.J. (1996) 'An interdisciplinary educational model for health professions students in a family practice center', *Nurse Educator*, vol 21, no 1, pp 27-31.

Lowry, C.F. (1987) 'Generic social work practice and family practice: students build a foundation for partnership', *Social Work in Health Care*, vol 12, no 2, pp 15-25.

McClelland, R. (1985) 'Joint degrees: do they strengthen or weaken the profession?', *Journal of Social Work Education*, vol 21, no 1, pp 20-6.

McCray, J. (1995) 'Twice the practitioner', *Nursing Times*, vol 91, no 49, Learn Disabil: pp 58-9.

Maidenburg, M.P. and Golick, T. (2001) 'Developing or enhancing interdisciplinary programs: a model for teaching collaboration', *Professional Development: The International Journal of Continuing Social Work Education*, vol 4, no 2, pp 15-24.

Manthorpe, J. (2000) 'Developing carers' contributions to social work training', *Social Work Education*, vol 19, no 1, pp 19-27.

Miller, C., Freeman, M. and Ross, N. (2001) *Interprofessional Practice in Health and Social Care: Challenging the Shared Learning Agenda*, London: Arnold.

Morrison, J.D., Howard, J., Johnson, C., Navarro, F.J., Plachetka, B. and Bell, T. (1997) 'Strengthening neighborhoods by developing community networks', *Social Work*, vol 42, no 5, pp 527-34.

Parsloe, P. and Swift, P. (1997) 'Applying partnership to assessing social work students', in D. Crepaz-Keay (ed) *Working with Service Users in Social Work Education and Training in Social Work and Social Care*, London: CCETSW.

Patford, J. (2001) 'Educating for cross-disciplinary collaboration: present trends and future possibilities', *Australian Social Work*, vol 54, no 3, pp 73-82.

Pickering, I. and Mullender, A. (1991) 'Learning together', *Issues in Social Work Education*, vol 11, pp 92-100.

Pierpont, J.H., Pozzuto, R. and Powell, J.Y. (2001) 'Service learning and systems of care: teaching students to learn from clients', *Journal of Family Social Work*, vol 5, no 3, pp 79-93.

Powell, J., Dosser, D., Handron, D., McCammon, S., Evans Temkin, M. and Kaufman, M. (1999) 'Challenges of interdisciplinary collaboration: a faculty consortium's initial attempts to model collaborative practice', *Journal of Community Practice*, vol 6, no 2, pp 27-48.

Preston-Shoot, M. (1989) 'A contractual approach to practice teaching', *Social Work Education*, vol 8, no 3, pp 3-15.

Russell, K.M. and Hymans, D. (1999) 'Interprofessional education for undergraduate students', *Public Health Nursing*, vol 16, no 4, pp 254-62.

Sable, M.R., Larrivee, L.S. and Gayer, D. (2001) 'Problem-based learning: opportunities and barriers for training interdisciplinary health care teams', *Journal of Teaching in Social Work*, vol 21, nos 3-4, pp 217-34.

Scheyett, A. and Diehl, M.J. (2004) 'Walking our talk in social work education: partnering with consumers of mental health services', *Social Work Education*, vol 23, no 4, pp 435-50.

Shardlow, S. (2000) 'Partnership with service users', in M. Daview (ed) *The Blackwell Encyclopaedia of Social Work*, Oxford: Blackwell.

Simoni, P.S. (2000) 'Social work graduate students' beliefs regarding responsibilities of professional nursing', *The Journal of Nursing Education*, vol 39, no 4, pp 188-91.

Sims, D. (1999) 'Education: joint training in learning disability nursing and social work', *British Journal of Community Nursing*, vol 4, no 6, pp 303-8.

Sklar, R. and Torczyner, J. (1991) 'Lawyers and social workers: a new joint Law-MSW degree program at McGill University', *Canadian Social Work Review/Revue Canadienne de Service Social*, vol 8, no 1, pp 97-105.

Tendler, D. and Metzger, K. (1978) 'Training in prevention: an educational model for social work students', *Social Work in Health Care*, vol 4, no 2, pp 221-31.

Tew, J., Townend, M., Hendry, S., Ryan, D., Glynn, T. and Clark, M. (2003) *On the Road to Partnership? User Involvement in Education and Training in the West Midlands*, Redditch: NIMHE West Midlands Regional Development Centre.

Tope, R. (1996) *Integrated Interdisciplinary Learning Between the Health and Social Care Professions: A Feasibility Study*, Cardiff: University of Wales.

Torkington, C., Lymbery, M., Millward, A., Murfin, M. and Richell, B. (2002) 'Research into practice – shared practice learning project', *Community Care*, 10 October, p 46.

Torkington, C., Lymbery, M., Millward, A., Murfin, M. and Richell, B. (2003) 'Shared practice learning: social work and district nurse students learning together', *Social Work Education*, vol 22, no 2, pp 165-75.

Torkington, C., Lymbery, M., Millward, A., Murfin, M. and Richell, B. (2004) 'The impact of shared practice learning on the quality of assessment carried out by social work and district nurse students', *Learning in Health and Social Care*, vol 3, no 1, pp 26-36.

Tracy, E.M. and Pine, B.A. (2000) 'Child welfare education and training: future trends and influences', *Child Welfare*, vol 79, no 1, pp 93-113.

Trevillion, S. and Bedford, L. (2003) 'Utopianism and pragmatism in interprofessional education', *Social Work Education*, vol 22, no 2, pp 215-27.

Tucker, S. (2003) 'Interprofessional education: a curriculum response to work with children and young people', *Children & Society*, vol 17, no 2, pp 137-48.

Whittington, C. (2003) *Learning for Collaborative Practice With Other Professions and Agencies: A Study to Inform Development of the Degree in Social Work*, London: Department of Health.

Additional references

Argyris, C. and Schon, D.A. (1974) *Theory in Practice: Increasing Personal Effectiveness*, San Francisco, CA: Jossey Bass.

Fielding, M., Bragg, S., Craig, J., Cunningham, I., Eraut, M., Gillinson, S., Horne, M., Robinson, C. and Thorp, J. (2005) *Factors Influencing the Transfer of Good Practice*, Nottingham: DfES Publications.

Glasby, J. and Lester, H. (2004) 'Cases for change in mental health: partnership working in mental health services', *Journal of Interprofessional Care*, vol 18, no 1, pp 11-16.

Joseph Rowntree Foundation (2005) 'User involvement in research: building on experience and developing standards', *Findings*, 0175, April, York: Joseph Rowntree Foundation.

Levin, E. (2004) *Involving Service Users and Carers in Social Work Education*, London: Social Care Institute for Excellence.

Parsloe, P. (1990) 'Social work education in the year 2000', *International Social Work*, vol 33, no 1, pp 13-25.

Polyani, M. (1967) *The Tacit Dimension*, New York, NY: Doubleday.

Robinson, C. and Sebba, J. (2004) *A Review of Research and Evaluation to Inform the Development of the New Postgraduate Professional Development Programme*, London: TTA.

Schon, D. (1987) *Educating the Reflective Practitioner*, San Francisco, CA: Jossey-Bass.

Social Work Education (2004) vol 23, no 2.

Social Work Education (2005) vol 24, no 4.

Appendix 1:
Technical appendix and search strategies

Method

The search strategy

The research review team developed the search strategy in consultation with Esther Coren (EPPI-Centre).

A few relevant terms were first identified for trial input into ASSIA, Medline and PsycInfo, chosen as a small, relatively representative sample of the databases (as between them they cover material from the social sciences, medicine and psychology). Further terms were identified within the citations returned by this process, and, where trialling them revealed that they were useful to the search strategy, they were included within it. This method provided a core search strategy that could serve as a basis for different team members to start from when searching the databases. The strategy was modified during searching on each individual database, to take account of the varying descriptor terms used to classify citations and to allow adaptations to be made. Introducing this flexibility into our search strategy enabled us to tailor it to the disciplinary orientation, classificatory system and level of sophistication of each database.

Databases

The choice of databases to search was determined by SCIE's guidance on systematic reviewing. The databases included in the search were:

Database	Database name in full
ASSIA	Applied Social Sciences Index and Abstracts
BEI	British Education Index
CareData	
CINAHL	Cumulative Index to Nursing and Allied Health Literature
Cochrane	
C2-SPECTR	Campbell Collaboration Social, Psychological, Educational and Criminological Trials Register
Dissertation Abstracts	
ERIC	Educational Resources Information Center
HMIC: KFND HMIC: DHZZ	Health Management Information Consortium
IBSS	International Bibliography of the Social Sciences
Medline	
PsycInfo	
SIGLE	System for Information on Grey Literature in Europe
Social Services Abstracts Social Work Abstracts Sociological Abstracts	
SSCI	Social Sciences Citations Index

ZETOC and Wilson Social Science Abstracts were not searched as initial investigation suggested that the amount of useful material they would provide would not justify the time taken to search them. It was also decided to use the SSCI rather than Social Sci Search, as suggested in the guidance, as it has similar coverage and was felt to be more useful. An attempt was made to search C2-SPECTR, but initial trialling revealed no relevant material, so the full search strategy was not used.

Handsearching

The *Journal of Social Work Education* and the *British Journal of Social Work* were handsearched.

Website searching

The following websites were searched in the course of the review:

www.sosig.ac.uk/social_welfare/ (Social Science Information Gateway)

http://brs.leeds.ac.uk/~beiwww/beirc.htm (British Education Internet Resource Catalogue)

http://sumsearch.uthscsa.edu/cgi-bin/

www.jisc.ac.uk/index.cfm?name=rg_social_main (the Joint Information Systems Committee Resource Guide for Social Sciences)

http://edina.ac.uk/ (JISC-funded national datacentre)

www.policyhub.gov.uk/ (developed by the Cabinet Office Government Social Research Unit)

No relevant documentation in addition to that which had been obtained by the other methods was discovered through this approach.

Screening, keywording and data extraction

The abstracts of all citations retrieved (4,654, including duplicates) were read to screen for relevance. This was done by applying the following inclusion/exclusion criteria to determine whether or not the full reference should be sent for:

- citations included must focus on social work education
- citations included must focus on qualifying education

- citations included must focus on partnership (see sections 1.4 and 2.1.3)
- citations included must be in the English language.

These criteria were decided on in order to limit the scope of the review to manageable proportions without omitting the most centrally relevant literature, although the team recognised that by doing so material of interest would inevitably be excluded, such as literature in languages other than English, literature focusing on partnership education in professions other than social work, etc. Applying these reduced to 638 (including duplicates) the number of citations to be considered.

Following initial screening, further discussions took place with SCIE, clarifying whether the terms of the review remit were to include literature on institutional partnership arrangements facilitating social work education, or whether they were limited to the teaching, learning and assessment of partnership work. The latter, narrower, focus was agreed on. Clarification was also received from SCIE at this point, that papers about interprofessional education should be included in the review only in so far as they considered partnership work explicitly. As a result further citations were excluded on the basis of abstracts, yielding a core of 223 unique citations from electronic databases, with an additional 37 gathered through handsearching of key journals.

The next stage was to read all of the included publications successfully obtained by the review team (235/260), with a view to serving two purposes. The first was further to re-apply the same inclusion criteria, this time on scrutiny of full texts; a further 116 publications were excluded as a result, leaving 119 publications, concerning 109 studies, included in total. The second purpose was to codify key information about each of the included studies, in order to provide an overview 'map' of the research informing this review. The keywording system used appears in Appendix 2. It was adapted by the team from the generic keywording format designed by the EPPI-Centre for use with educational research studies. The revised version was designed to incorporate both generic and review-specific information, explicitly addressing partnership in social work education. All 119 publications included in the review were keyworded using this format. The information gathered in this way provided the data for the overview research map, discussed in section 2.2.

A small selection of studies included in the research review was ultimately selected for data extraction, providing an in-depth assessment of the quality and relevance of each study to the review question. The main criterion applied to select them for detailed scrutiny was that the work was sufficiently empirical, and the methodology reported in sufficient detail, to be capable of subjection to data extraction. In addition, the inclusion criteria relating to partnership work and interprofessional education were all applied more stringently at this stage, since unlike the other inclusion criteria these were more open to interpretation. Thirteen studies were selected for data extraction and in-depth review; a further 12 were identified as eligible for similar scrutiny, but unfortunately this could not be achieved within the available time and resources. Data extraction included rigorous judgements of validity, reliability, user engagement and quality of the research design, execution and reporting. The review team used the generic EPPI-Centre data extraction strategy, with minor modifications made to reflect the focus of the review. Full discussion of the in-depth research review appears in section 2.3.

Reliability and quality assurance

Reliability was ensured by checking agreement between team members and by an external quality assessor at every stage, as shown in the table below:

Stage of process	Proportion double-checked	Proportion quality assessed externally
Screening of abstracts	10%	10%
Keywording	17%	10%
Data extraction	100%	25%

Where there was disagreement, the following occurred:

Screening of abstracts: it was decided that we would err on the side of inclusiveness in any dispute, and only exclude citations where this was agreed. In the event it did not arise; there was no significant disagreement, since each researcher independently erred on the side of inclusion.

Keywording: disagreements were sent to the EPPI-Centre quality assessor for arbitration. This was in addition to the 10% sample that was quality assessed.

Data extraction: where there was disagreement, the two reviewers met to discuss the issue. If agreement could not be reached, it would be referred to the external assessor for arbitration.

Results

The table below shows the number of citations obtained by the search strategies reported above: before any screening took place, after initial screening took place, and when the inclusion criteria were further refined leading to more citations being screened out:

Database	Total citations retrieved by search strategy[a]	Total citations included after initial screening[a]	Total citations included after refining inclusion criteria
ASSIA	248	90	42
BEI	9	0	0
CareData	402	38	27
CINAHL	862	95	68
Cochrane	9	0	0
Dissertation Abstracts	77	4	4
ERIC	101	10	2
HMIC: DHZZ	89	19	14
HMIC: KFND	20	12	9
IBSS	100	5	3
Medline	177	85	46
PsycInfo	228	62	23
SIGLE	94	16	14
Social Services Abstracts	792	138	63
Social Work Abstracts	348	19	10
Sociological Abstracts	94	5	3
SSCI	1,004	40	20
Handsearching	–	–	4
Identified from Bibliographies	–	–	33
Website searching	–	–	0

Note: [a] Because of the numbers involved, these figures have not been filtered to take duplicates into account

The table below shows the breakdown of the total citations into unique and duplicate records selected on the basis of abstracts, once the screening and refinement of inclusion criteria had taken place. Note that the first row of total figures gives the sum of the citations found across all the databases, and therefore counts duplicate citations each time they appear. The row below gives the number of actual citations found, filtering out duplicate entries.

Database	Total citations	Duplicates	Unique citations
ASSIA	42	33	9
BEI	0	0	0
CareData	27	21	6
CINAHL	68	24	44
Cochrane	0	0	0
Dissertation Abstracts	4	0	4
ERIC	2	0	2
HMIC: DHZZ	14	8	6
HMIC: KFND	9	5	4
IBSS	3	2	1
Medline	44	21	23
PsycInfo	23	18	5
SIGLE	14	3	11
Social Services Abstracts	63	40	23
Social Work Abstracts	10	9	1
Sociological Abstracts	3	3	0
SSCI	20	13	7
Total	346	200	146
Total when each duplicate is counted only once	260	114	146

The final figures for references that we obtained or sought to obtain are as follows:

Outcomes for identified references	Number
Included in research review (keyworded)	119
Excluded	116
Unable to obtain	25
Total	260
Data extracted	12

Flow chart of research review process
Databases searched:

ASSIA	CareData	Cochrane	CINAHL	ERIC
HMIC	Medline	PsycInfo	SIGLE	SSCI
Social services Abstracts	C2-SPECTR	IBSS	Dissertation Abstracts	Social Work Abstracts

4,654 citations obtained[a]

↓

Inclusion/exclusion criteria applied
638 citations[a]

↓

Inclusion/exclusion criteria refined further
(following consultation with SCIE)
223 unique citations

↓

+37 citations discovered
through handsearching
and in references

260 total unique citations

235 publications successfully obtained
116 publications excluded on full reading as not
meeting inclusion criteria

119 citations (109 studies) included in research review

↓

25 citations (24 studies) potential for data extraction

13 studies included in data extraction

Note: [a] Duplicates have not been filtered out where marked.

Appendix 2:
Keywording strategy

A.1 Linked reports[a]	Not Linked Linked
A.2 Identification of report (or reports)[a]	Citation Handsearch Electronic database Contact Unknown
A.3 Status[a]	Published In press Unpublished
A.4 Location of study[a]	UK USA Europe Australia Other (please specify) Not specified
A.5 Partnership work in social work education: topic	Partnership work with users/carers (academic curriculum) User/carer involvement in teaching partnership work Partnership work with users/carers (practice learning) User/carer involvement in assessing partnership work (includes student selection) Partnership work with users/carers (non-specific focus) Interprofessional education with partnership work focus (shared academic curriculum)

A.5: topic continued	Interprofessional education with partnership work focus (shared practice learning) Academic curriculum (for social work students only) with interprofessional partnership work focus Practice learning (for social work students only) with interprofessional partnership work focus General/non-specific focus Interprofessional partnership work focus (for social work students only) Dual qualifying education for 'joint practitioners' Other (please specify)
A.6 Partnership work as curriculum content: includes academic or practice curricula	Social work student and service user/carer Social work student and other professional/other student Social work student and educator/assessor Social work educator/assessor and educator/assessor from other discipline Educator/assessor and stakeholder (including service users/carers) University and stakeholder Other (please specify) Not applicable
A.7 Partnership work as practice competence	Social work student and service user/carer Social work student and other professional/other student Social work student and educator/assessor Other (please specify) Not applicable

A.8 Partnership in organisation/ process of education about partnership work	Social work student and service user/carer Social work student and other professional/other student Social work student and educator/assessor Social work educator/assessor and educator/assessor from other discipline Educator/assessor and stakeholder (including service users/carers) University and stakeholder Other (please specify) Not applicable
A.9 Academic educational process focus	Teaching Learning Assessment Student selection Other (please specify) Not specified Not applicable
A.10 Practice educational process focus	Teaching Learning assessment Student selection Other (please specify) Not specified Not applicable
A.11 Social work area	General childcare or family support Children looked after Elderly Learning disability Youth justice Disability Mental health Child protection Generic Other Not specified
A.12 Programme/ course name and location	Details (please complete)

A.13 Programme/ course type	Details (please complete)
A.14 Focus population (all papers)	Service user as course advisor Service user as consumer of service Service user as assessor of student Employers (social work agency – management level) Practitioners Practice teachers HEI educators HEI (establishment) Students Other (please specify)
A.15 Research population (empirical studies only)	Service user as course advisor Service user as consumer of service Service user as assessor of student Employers (social work agency – management level) Practitioners Practice teachers HEI educators HEI (establishment) Students Other (please specify)
A.16 Academic educational setting: discipline	Social work/care only Multidisciplinary Other (please specify) Not specified Not applicable
A.17 Academic educational setting: location	HEI Tertiary education Workplace based Other (please specify) Not specified Not applicable

A.18 Practice educational setting: discipline	Social work/care only Multidisciplinary Other (please specify) Not specified Not applicable
A.19 Practice educational setting: location	Statutory sector Voluntary sector Residential Secure environments Other (please specify) Not specified Not applicable
A.20 Suitability for data extraction	Yes Possible (please specify) No

Notes: [a] Items A.1-A.4: EPPI-Centre core keywords
Items A.5-A.20: SCIE partnership review specific keywords
HEI: Higher Education Institute

Appendix 3: Data extracted studies

Study	Aims of the study	Intervention	Study design	Findings and conclusions
Carpenter and Hewstone (1996)	Study (two linked studies) aim to describe and evaluate shared learning programme for medical and Social Work (SW) students, designed to improve attitudes and knowledge of skills, roles and duties of each other and increase ability to work collaboratively	'Shared Learning Programme' for medics and social workers (with some health visitor and nursing students involved in one cohort). Took place over 2.5 days during one week, for final year medics and final year Masters Social Work (MSW) or Certificate in Qualification in Social Work (CQSW) students	Variant of a 'one-group' pre-test post-test design, with change measured using Analysis of Variance (ANOVA). This provides a test for the presence of interaction between time, ie from the beginning to the end of the programme and group, ie doctors and social workers	Programme demonstrated how attitudes can be changed and knowledge increased among qualifying social workers and doctors that authors argue are necessary for cooperation in practice. But: • in some cases (19%) it was aversive and attitudes worsened • no evidence that attitude change will be lasting, since no long-term follow • unable to tell whether particular features of the programme design were what made it effective. Shared learning does not remove all the barriers to interprofessional cooperation, many of which are structural

Study	Aims of the study	Intervention	Study design	Findings and conclusions
Colarossi and Forgey (2006: forthcoming)	Evaluates effectiveness of Interprofessional Education (IPE) in domestic violence for law and social work students in terms of knowledge about domestic violence in general, interdisciplinary knowledge, changing attitudes	Domestic Violence: Law and Social Work: an interdisciplinary course lasting 14 weeks at Fordham University's Interdisciplinary Center for Family and Child Advocacy, USA. Interdisciplinary module in final year of qualifying programme	Prospective, controlled study, comparing experimental (48) and control (45) groups of combined law and social work students, evaluating outcomes of IPE. Measures were knowledge of and attitudes towards domestic violence and interdisciplinary work	Gains from interdisciplinary learning of social workers and lawyers on: • knowledge of domestic violence • attitudes towards domestic violence. But attitudes towards interdisciplinary work did not improve. Conclusion underplays this latter finding – significant difference over time between the experimental and control groups due to worsening attitudes of the controls? Several caveats given re external and internal validity, and re extrapolations that might be made from change in attitudes/knowledge

Study	Aims of the study	Intervention	Study design	Findings and conclusions
Fineberg et al (2004)	Evaluate educational model in the development of collaborative understanding among medical and social work students – increase understanding of mutual professional and interdisciplinary collaborative roles	Module entitled: Multidisciplinary Care Tools: Teamwork and Family Conferencing in Palliative Care. Beth Israel Deaconess Medical Centre, California Interdisciplinary module, in palliative care, for second (final) year MSW students, and third/fourth year medics	Intervention consisted of 4-week experiential exercises. Control group received written material on the same topic. Students' perceived understanding of professional roles and interdisciplinary collaboration measured pre-training, post-training and three-month follow-up	Intervention resulted in an increase in perceived understanding of professional roles, which maintained at three-month follow-up, and significantly greater than change in the control group. Students valued the intervention. The results of study suggest professional socialisation in multidisciplinary work can effectively be influenced early in the socialisation of healthcare professionals. Limitations acknowledged of small sample size, non-random group assignments, participants being volunteers, and above all lack of measurement of actual as opposed to perceived knowledge of professional roles

Study	Aims of the study	Intervention	Study design	Findings and conclusions
Hyer et al (2000)	To provide additional construct validity for an existing instrument (Attitudes Toward Health Care Teams Scale: ATHCT) with student (medicine, nursing, social work and allied health) rather than practitioner groups	Geriatric Interdisciplinary Team Training (GITT) programme – national initiative to prepare professionals to work on geriatric interdisciplinary teams. Average 10 MSW students receive 148–1,036 hours including placement. Targets social work, nursing & medics. Study tested construct validity of Heinemann et al (1999) ATHCT Scale, assessing 'attitudes, knowledge and skills about teams and team behaviour'	Study examined construct validity of ATHCT Scale with 913 graduate students (medics, social work, nursing, pharmacy and allied professions) on interdisciplinary geriatric training in 8 centres across US	The ATHCT Scale revalidated with student healthcare teams – noted to be a useful means for assessing interdisciplinary training in geriatrics, as well as important means of communicating with trainees about components of team care. Changed labels on scales: quality of care>team efficiency costs/benefits of team care>team value physician centrality>shared learning. Acknowledged that generalisations beyond the sample limited, but the validation of the ATHCT Scale presented in this article strengthens the case for using this instrument

Study	Aims of the study	Intervention	Study design	Findings and conclusions
Jackson and Morris (1994)	Central Council for Education and Training in Social Work (CCETSW) commissioned Family Rights Group (FRG) to review the teaching of partnership in family and childcare work to qualifying social workers. Survey of course provision, practical means of providing qualifying teaching about the philosophy and ...	No specific programme – research based on seven (and some details of an eighth) unnamed social work qualifying programmes: 4 graduate, 3 non-graduate, 2 employment-based, 5 college-based. Focus on concepts of partnership, coverage in the course and placements ...	Exploratory study of seven social work programmes across England and Wales to identify the concepts, methods and tools developed for knowledge and skills in working in partnership with families. Students, programme tutors and practice teachers were asked to complete questionnaires and contribute to ...	Difficulties in defining partnership, many students didn't answer this question. Understanding needed of how oppression can create barriers to partnership work. Authors suggest clarity of definition needed to teach and enable students, practice teachers and tutors to evaluate. Partnership generally integrated throughout the teaching programme. Programmes which linked teaching of partnership with practice learning – more effective. Child protection well covered, residential services not. Four areas identified for future: limited reference made by students to research; absence of specific guidance for partnership skills in CCETSW material; lack of inking between oppression and working in partnership; lack of coverage of residential services...

Study	Aims of the study	Intervention	Study design	Findings and conclusions
Jackson and Morris (1994) continued	... accompanying skills required for working in partnership with families	... and use of research in the course	... a tape-recorded discussion	... Recommendations: define partnership; see process of negotiating placement as partnership opportunity; make greater use of consumer input including in assessment of placements; reconsider whether partnership should be addressed more explicitly rather than losing or diluting it through integration

Study	Aims of the study	Intervention	Study design	Findings and conclusions
Johnson (2003)	To survey the opinions of first year health and social care students and gain insights in an undergraduate interprofessional module at an English university. Role of interprofessional curriculum in influencing attitudes to collaborative learning	Interprofessional Module in first year of 10 different qualifying programmes at University of West of England. IPE programme has further modules, one in each year (this research focuses on Module 1). Students drawn from nursing, diagnostic imaging, learning disabilities nursing, mental health nursing, midwifery, ...	Cross-sectional, single time point study, based on standard university evaluation questionnaires on student opinions, beliefs and attitudes about an IPE module. 65 evaluation forms, drawn from 205 (31%) returned of total possible of 656 students (so 10% of overall student population)....	Views of first year health and social care students undertaking IPE module in first six weeks of their training – well received by many – enlightening, but both enquiry-based learning and the relevance of IPE were a mystery to many others. Strong theme of tension between IPE and uniprofessional studies in terms of relevance, resources, demands, status. Confused and anxious about the assessment tasks – led to revision of the guidelines. Author argues for early introduction of IPE into professional training, but that 'strategies to enhance its perceived relevance and clarity as part of the professional programmes should accompany early introduction'.

Study	Aims of the study	Intervention	Study design	Findings and conclusions
Johnson (2003) continued		...occupational therapy (OT), physiotherapy, radiotherapy and SW	...Qualitative comments and quantitative (Likert Scale) data	

Study	Aims of the study	Intervention	Study design	Findings and conclusions
Julia and Kondrat (2000)	Extent to which social work research methodology in MSW programmes in US encourage active involvement in process of research by the people whose lives are being studied	Not applicable – no intervention as such. Survey based on 75/121 MSW programmes in US	Descriptive study using content analysis of printed syllabi of MSW research methods courses in US. Cross-sectional, based on 75 responding of the 121 total MSW programmes, academic year 1995-96	Graduate social work research syllabi and textbooks offer little attention either to specific methods of participatory research or to concepts related to empowerment and collaboration in the research process. Use only documented/recorded accounts of syllabi so might have missed what may be included but isn't apparent on paper. Conclude need to include participatory forms of research alongside more conventional research methods taught to social work students

Study	Aims of the study	Intervention	Study design	Findings and conclusions
Kane (1976)	Survey of schools of social work in US to see what they are doing to meet the present and future need for teamwork skills. Including curricular areas, how much and how far is IPE in joint or social work only courses	Not applicable – no intervention as such. Survey of MSW programmes in US and Canada in 1974 looked at coverage of interprofessional team work in MSW curricula	Descriptive, cross-sectional survey (using postal questionnaire) and analysis of interprofessional team work/ collaborative teaching on all MSW programmes in US and Canada, 1974	Most schools of social work gave little attention to interprofessional teamwork (16:64 schools had no content in the area at all). 50% of programmes claim strong emphasis on IPE in practicum; 34% slight, 13% none. Teamwork takes variety of forms on MSW curricula. General association between teaching and learning of teamwork on MSWs and health-related courses – either on joint courses, or electives on social work in health settings, or both. Objective of IPE is to enable students to establish and keep own professional identities but develop collaborative teamwork, ie 'combined understandings but separate talents' (p 237)

Study	Aims of the study	Intervention	Study design	Findings and conclusions
Pollard et al (2006: forth-coming)	Explore effects of a prequalifying IPE in each year of study. Students from 10 professional disciplines – including self-assessment of their communication and teamwork skills, and their attitudes to collaborative learning and working	Interprofessional programme, involving module in each year of degree course. Serves qualifying undergraduate degree (or nursing diploma) programmes in a range of 10 disciplines at the University of the West of England	Longitudinal evaluation of effectiveness of recent IPE initiative at an Higher Education Institution (HEI). Prospective study, examines student cohort (initially 852), from 10 professional programmes. Self-assessment questionnaires on communication and teamwork, attitudes to collaborative learning and work	Negative attitudes displayed by most students towards interprofessional interaction, but positive towards IPE. Older, more experienced students held most negative views. Positive attitudes towards interprofessional learning and assessing own skills in communication and teamwork but accuracy of students' self-assessment questioned. Supports early IPE, which prevents the formation of stereotypes associated with uniprofessional education. No comparison group, so can't attribute changes to IPE confidently

Study	Aims of the study	Intervention	Study design	Findings and conclusions
Scheyett and Kim (2004)	To explore the effects of a facilitated dialogue process between consumers and MSW students aimed at shifting student attitudes towards consumers	MSW programme, University of North Carolina. One day (6 hours) facilitated dialogue workshop, between 10 first and second year MSW students, and 10 service users. Facilitated dialogue involves bringing together disparate groups to discuss challenging issues	Evaluation of changes in social work students' attitudes following a one-day intervention in facilitated dialogue. Pre and post-tests on three attitude scales, info on prior experience of consumers and interviews afterwards to collect students' insights and informally from consumers	Changes in attitudes significantly positive on all three scales. Before 'dialogue' some students had negative views of consumers based on prior personal or professional experience. Changes in attitudes towards consumers included stigma and relationships, empathy, understanding, awareness of consumer strength and skills. Reported intentions to change practice. The model honours consumers' experience and wisdom by inviting them to participate in a process that will shape future social workers – true partnership with consumers in a strengths-based framework

Study	Aims of the study	Intervention	Study design	Findings and conclusions
Shor and Sykes (2002)	To evaluate use of 'Structured Dialogue' (SD) in work with social work trainees on BSW. To learn about students' perceptions of people with mental illness prior to structured dialogue and changes following meeting.... To learn about the thoughts, feelings and dilemmas evoked by the meetings	'Structured Dialogue', Bachelor in Social Work (BSW) programme, Hebrew University, Jerusalem. One-off practice centred classes with BSW students. SD sessions last 1.5 hours. Two mental health service users 'present' at each session, one as facilitator gives background to SD and user group and second one tells own personal ...	Descriptive and prospective study, evaluating impact of BSW SD initiative, on student attitudes/ experiences and understanding. Intervention. No comparison or control groups. Post-test experiences of all 185 students and pre plus post-test attitudes of 65 of these in 5 of the 15 classes involved using ...	Qualitative Differentiation and Trust and Meliorism were not significantly different post-test to pre-test. At both stages, students expressed non-judgemental attitudes re people with mental illness. Post-test students saw less differences between those with mental illness and the rest of us – correlated significantly with perceived benefit of SDs for increasing understanding re mental illness. Qualitative data suggest attitude measures not indicative of the actual extent of student awareness/understanding of mental illness. Students felt SD experience contributed to their learning re mentally ill people, and important to continue meetings. Presenters (users) found SD experience valuable – improved confidence and self-esteem, empowering, supportive of ...

Study	Aims of the study	Intervention	Study design	Findings and conclusions
Shor and Sykes (2002) continued		...story. Facilitator opens meeting for discussion (reversal of usual hierarchy)	... questionnaires – some open-ended and some Likert-scaled questions. Feedback from some or all presenters also obtained	...recovery. SD is example of experiential model that can enable students to interact with and learn from people with mental illness in an open, non-threatening situation

Study	Aims of the study	Intervention	Study design	Findings and conclusions
Whittington and Bell (2001)	Inform the agenda for the new social work curricula. Identify those with whom social workers are in contact, skills needed, usefulness of shared training in developing these and differences between CQSW versus Certificate in Social Service (CSS)	Not applicable – no intervention. Survey of sample from all qualifying social work programmes in CCETSW's London and South East region, students qualifying in 1990. Included CQSW programmes – HEI-based CSS programme – part-time Further Education college-based or workplace training course for social care workers in post	Cross-sectional descriptive study, based on postal questionnaire to 752 practitioners in one region, a year after qualification (CSS and CQSW). Study sample 489 respondents, working in all social work sectors, statutory, voluntary and probation. Explores shared learning	Gaps in preparation through qualifying education identified by social workers to work with wide range of other organisations and professions. Perceived selves to have been well prepared to work with other social workers. Perceived their own roles to be poorly understood by other professions, especially doctors and others least likely to be involved in shared learning. Practice learning and post-qualifying experience perceived as contributing most to interprofessional competences. CSS rated selves better prepared than CQSW

Study	Aims of the study	Intervention	Study design	Findings and conclusions
Wikler (1979)	Investigate way in which consumer perspective on interviewing differs from that of the faculty and trainees. Involve the consumer in training as an active participant	University of Wisconsin School of Social Work, Madison, USA, 1979. No formal name given. Intervention described as a 'consumer's day' training experience for social work students. Parents of 'mentally retarded children' invited to contribute to training by being interviewed by students, observing students interviewing others and giving feedback	Descriptive study of process and experiences of involving consumers in training day for social work students, providing content of own experiences in interview and feedback on interview. Ranking of which skills most important	Importance of involving consumers of services in training of social work students – parents and professionals agreed on importance of some interviewing skills and disagreed on others. Acknowledged parents' strengths and coping abilities. Parents and faculty agreed that most important feature of an interview is that the interviewer should 'really listen'

Appendix 4:
Practice Survey letters

Letter 1: To social work programme directors

Dear

Re: Teaching, learning and assessing partnership work in social work educa-tion: A Knowledge Review for the Social Care Institute for Excellence

We have been commissioned by SCIE (Social Care Institute for Excellence) to conduct the above Knowledge Review and Analytical Report on teaching, learning and assessing partnership work in social work education. The study will consist of a Research Review and a Practice Survey. I am writing to you to seek your help with the Practice Survey.

You will be aware that 'partnership' features in different ways in the regulatory documentation for the new degree in social work: as a com-petence in the National Occupational Standards; as a topic that students must learn about in the university; and as an element of organisational structures to support learning and teaching.

Our aim is to map current and emergent arrangements for partnership work in the new degree (at undergraduate and postgraduate levels), and to identify examples of 'best practice'. The first stage of our research is to conduct a national survey of practice and develop a profile of current practice. The second stage is for a sample of HEI providers to be inter-viewed by telephone, seeking in particular examples of 'best practice'. Finally, we will establish focus groups of stakeholders on 5 HEI sites to further explore 'best practice' issues. Each stage is planned in consulta-tion with our project Stakeholder Group.

To assist with the first stage of mapping the profile of practice, we are seeking a copy of your relevant programme documentation, in particular your Programme and Module Handbooks. We think it might be easier for you to give us information about your partnership work in this way rather than respond to a complex questionnaire. We hope that you agree with this! We will ensure that information provided by you is anonymised and is confidential to the project team.

We would be very grateful if you could forward your relevant documentation to the above address. If you require any further information please do not hesitate to contact us.

Elaine Keep, Research Officer
Professor Imogen Taylor, Research Director

Letter 2: To service users as potential focus group participants

Teaching, learning and assessing partnership work in social work education: A Knowledge Review for the Social Care Institute for Excellence

Dear Service User/Carer,

We are a small research team from the School of Social Work and Social Care, University of Sussex. Our team includes academics, service users and students. We are carrying out a 'Practice Survey' of the teaching, learning and assessment of partnership work in social work education at qualifying level. We are inviting you to help with our research and take part in a focus group interview with an academic researcher and a service user.

We have selected five Universities where our initial research suggests that there are examples of good practice in the learning, teaching and assessing of partnership work. We are now seeking your views about such work at the London Metropolitan University.

We are asking for about one hour of your time. We will reimburse you following the interview at the hourly rate that you would be paid by the

London Metropolitan University. We will also provide cash payment for any travel expenses at the time of the interview.

We have designed some interview questions to guide the discussion. With your consent, the discussion will be tape-recorded. We will ask you to complete a consent form when you meet. The taped interview will be transcribed. Individuals will not be identified in the final report. All tapes will be destroyed once the project is completed.

If you are in agreement to meeting with us, could you please contact Elaine Keep, our Research Officer, at this address? Elaine's phone no. is 01273 872623. Elaine will take your number when you ring and phone you back right away. Or, you may prefer to email Elaine at E.M.E.Keeep@sussex.ac.uk

If you have any questions, Elaine will be happy to answer them. We look forward to hearing from you

Professor Imogen Taylor
Project Director

Letter 3: To students as potential focus group participants

Teaching, learning and assessing partnership work in social work education: A Knowledge Review for the Social Care Institute for Excellence

Dear Student

We are a small research team from the School of Social Work and Social Care, University of Sussex. Our team includes academics, service users and students. We are carrying out a 'Practice Survey' of the teaching, learning and assessment of partnership work in social work education at qualifying level. We are inviting you to help with our research and take part in a focus group interview of about 5-6 students with an academic researcher and hopefully University of Sussex students from our team if the proposed meeting time is suitable to them.

We have selected five Universities where our initial research suggests that there are examples of good practice in the learning, teaching and assessing of partnership work. We are now seeking your views about such work at London Metropolitan University.

We are asking you for about one hour of your time. We will reimburse you following the interview with a book token worth £15.00. We will also provide cash payment at the time for any travel expenses to the interview.

We have designed some interview questions to guide the discussion. With your consent, the discussion will be tape-recorded. We will ask you to complete a consent form, which is attached to this letter, and give it to the interviewer when you meet. The taped interview will be transcribed. Individuals will not be identified in the final report. All tapes will be destroyed once the project is completed.

If you have any questions or concerns, please contact Elaine Keep, our Research Officer, by email at E.M.E.Keeep@sussex.ac.uk

We hope to meet you soon.

Professor Imogen Taylor
Project Director

Appendix 5:
Consent form for focus group participants

Consent

I agree to take part in this research. I have read the statement from the research team and I understand that the discussion will be taped, the main themes summarised and the tape destroyed after the research is completed.

NAME:

ADDRESS:

TELEPHONE

EMAIL

Appendix 6:
Telephone interview schedule for Practice Survey (with HEIs)

Part 1

The first part of these questions is about classroom-based learning; we will then move to learning in practice settings.

We have reviewed the documentation you have sent us including (specify) and notice that....

You discuss partnership in your programme handbook but I could not find it in classroom-based modules (or vice versa)....

Can you give us an example of partnership working in design and delivery of the new degree on your programme?

Who is participating in the partnership?

Did this partnership exist prior to the new award?

Can you tell us about a specific example where your programme requires partnership working to be demonstrated?

Can you give us an example of partnership working in admissions to the new degree on your programme?

Who is participating in the partnership?

Did this partnership exist prior to the new award?

Can you give us an example of partnership working in assessment to the new degree on your programme?

Who is participating in the partnership?

Did this partnership exist prior to the new award?

Can you give us an example of partnership working in monitoring and review of the new degree on your programme?

Who is participating in the partnership?

Did this partnership exist prior to the new award?

(If relevant) We have been discussing the undergraduate programme – what is different in the Masters if anything?

Time frame implications?

Partnership work in context of research methods/dissertations?

Part 2

Now we want to think about partnership in practice settings.

eg GSCC Code of Practice, 6.7 requires workers to recognise and respect the roles and expertise of workers from other agencies and work in partnership with them.

Can you tell us about a specific example where your programme requires partnership working to be demonstrated?

I notice that you have not talked about service users/students/other professionals.

Part 3

Do you think that any of the examples that you have given us might demonstrate 'good' practice?

Say more about what you think are the qualities of good practice in educating students about partnership work.

Index

Other Knowledge Reviews available from SCIE

LEARNING AND TEACHING IN SOCIAL WORK EDUCATION: ASSESSMENT

Beth R. Crisp, Mark R. Anderson,
Joan Orme and Pam Green Lister
ISBN 1 904812 00 7
November 2003
Ordering code: KR01

THE ADOPTION OF LOOKED AFTER CHILDREN: A SCOPING REVIEW OF RESEARCH

Alan Rushton
ISBN 1 904812 01 5
November 2003
Ordering code: KR02

TYPES AND QUALITY OF KNOWLEDGE IN SOCIAL CARE

Ray Pawson, Annette Boaz,
Lesley Grayson, Andrew Long and
Colin Barnes
ISBN 1 904812 02 3
November 2003
Ordering code: KR03

INNOVATIVE, TRIED AND TESTED: A REVIEW OF GOOD PRACTICE IN FOSTERING

Clive Sellick and Darren Howell
ISBN 1 904812 03 1
November 2003
Ordering code: KR04

FOSTERING SUCCESS: AN EXPLORATION OF THE RESEARCH LITERATURE IN FOSTER CARE

Kate Wilson, Ian Sinclair, Claire Taylor,
Andrew Pithouse and Clive Sellick
ISBN 1 904812 04 X
January 2004
Ordering code: KR05

TEACHING AND LEARNING COMMUNICATION SKILLS IN SOCIAL WORK EDUCATION

Pamela Trevithick, Sally Richards,
Gillian Ruch and Bernard Moss
with Linda Lines and Oded Manor
ISBN 1 904812 12 0
May 2004
Ordering code: KR06

IMPROVING THE USE OF RESEARCH IN SOCIAL CARE PRACTICE

Isabel Walter, Sandra Nutley,
Janie Percy-Smith, Di McNeish and
Sarah Frost
ISBN 1 904812 13 9
June 2004
Ordering code: KR07

TEACHING, LEARNING AND ASSESSMENT OF LAW IN SOCIAL WORK EDUCATION

Suzy Braye and Michael Preston-Shoot with
Lesley-Ann Cull, Robert Johns
and Jeremy Roche
ISBN 1 904812 20 1
April 2005
Ordering code: KR08

LEARNING AND TEACHING IN SOCIAL WORK EDUCATION: TEXTBOOKS AND FRAMEWORKS ON ASSESSMENT

Beth R. Crisp, Mark R. Anderson,
Joan Orme and Pam Green Lister
ISBN 1 904812 21 x
April 2005
Ordering code: KR09

Join SCIE's update list

SCIE works with people and organisations throughout the social care sector to identify useful information, research and examples of good practice.

Using this information, we produce resources which evaluate practice in a particular area of social care, draw out key messages for good practice and identify areas where more research is needed to inform good practice.

Practitioners, researchers, service users and policy makers rely on SCIE's resources as a central and trusted point for evidence-based good practice guidance.

SCIE's work covers the breadth of social care including services for adults, children and families, participation, human resource development, social work education, e-learning and the use of knowledge in social care.

Visit www.scie.org.uk today, or fax this form to us at +44 (0)20 7089 6841.

Please enter your details here

Name

Job title

Organisation

Address

Telephone   Facsimile

Email

Please tick what areas of SCIE's work you are interested in:

☐ adult services
☐ children and families services
☐ e-learning
☐ electronic Library for Social Care
☐ human resource development
☐ knowledge in social care
☐ participation
☐ social work education

SCIE commissions out much of its work. If you are interested in applying for SCIE's commissions, please tick here ☐

Data protection

The information you provide on this booking form will be held on a database so that we can keep you up-to-date with relevant publications and other SCIE news. We will not pass your details on to any other company.

Please fill out the form overleaf and return to SCIE at:

Communications Team

Social Care Institute for Excellence

Goldings House

2 Hay's Lane

London SE1 2HB

or fax it to 020 7089 6841